45-95 BK Bud May 95

The European Community

An Essential Guide Toward Knowing and Understanding the EC

Mark A. Kauffman

The European Community

An Essential Guide Toward
Knowing and Understanding the EC

First Edition

Stone & Quill
P u b l i s h i n g

Published 1993
Printed in the United States of America
International Standard Book Number: 1-883377-16-1
Library of Congress Catalog Card Number: 93-84479

∞

The paper used in this publication meets
the minimum requirements of American National Standard
for Information Sciences—Permanence of Paper
for Printed Library Materials, ANZI Z39.48-1984.

Publisher's Cataloging in Publication
(Prepared by Quality Books Inc.)

Kauffman, Mark A., 1965—
    The European Community : an essential guide toward knowing
and understanding the EC / Mark A. Kauffman. -- 1st ed.
    p. cm.
    Includes index.
    Preassigned LCCN: 93-84479.
    ISBN 1-883377-16-1
    1. European Economic Community--History. 2. European Economic
Community--Politics and government. 3. European Economic Community
countries. 4. European Economic Community--Relations--European
Free Trade Association. 5. European Economic Community--Relations
--Europe, Eastern. I. Title

HC241.2.K38 1993   337.142
                               QB193-1089

Dedicated to the memory of my mother,
Linda Charlene Biggs,
the most caring parent imaginable,
and to Anne,
whose faith in me made this book possible.

Contents

Preface

When I first heard about the European Community and its efforts to transform Europe into a vast open market, I was astounded. How wonderful that the nations who were, not that long ago, embroiled in the most bloody conflict in history have now pulled together to nurture peace and prosperity. Though I've learned that the situation is really not quite that simple, the outcome, peace, still prevails. What struck me most profoundly about the European Community is how quickly and adamantly I found myself supporting it. Being an American, I am naturally inclined toward wishing to see the Community succeed. The nostalgia of the 13 original US colonies banding together to create what has become the world's most powerful nation, makes most Americans spontaneous advocates of the EC's concepts.

I believe the future holds both great challenges and great opportunities, and am convinced that success in the coming decades will revolve around understanding the changes in the world around us. World trends increasingly influence people's individual lives, and an understanding of them is becoming a necessity of modern life. Even the notion of career planning has drastically changed in the past decade, largely due to the influence of the global marketplace. No longer can one expect to gain employment at a large corporation, receive a handsome salary with annual raises and then retire 35 years later with a comfortable pension. Global competition has changed all that. But those who understand these changes are the ones most likely to recognize the new opportunities provided by them.

Today's shifts in the workplace and marketplace are similar in magnitude to the those of the Industrial Revolution, which caused incredible upheavals at the turn of the century. But just as new opportunities emerged for those who adopted the new ways then, so will they today. I hope the knowledge gained from this book will become a tiny part of the awareness that helps you successfully navigate the stormy waters of coming decades.

Acknowledgments

During the year that this book was written, certain people and organizations provided me with information and services that were essential to the project's success. I owe gratitude to the librarians at the EC Commission's permanent delegation in Geneva, Switzerland, as well as those at the University of Lausanne, Switzerland. I would especially like to thank Jim Buck for the time and effort he spent editing this book, and Anne Matzinger for her assistance with the book's graphics.

List of Acronyms

The following is a list of acronyms used in this book. Each acronym is also defined in the text when it is first used. Additional information regarding these terms may be found in the glossary at the back of the book, as well as in the index.

CAP	Common Agricuture Policy
CEN	European Committee for Standardization
Cenelec	European Committee for Electrotechnical Standardization
DG	Directorate General
EAGGF	European Agriculture Guidance and Guarantee Fund
EC	European Community
ECB	European Central Bank
ECSC	European Coal and Steel Community
ECU	European Currency Unit
EEA	European Economic Area
EEC	European Economic Community
EES	European Economic Space
EFTA	European Free Trade Association
EIB	European Investment Bank
EMI	European Monetary Institute
EMS	European Monetary System
EMU	European Monetary Union
ERDF	European Regional Development Fund
ERM	Exchange Rate Mechanism
ESCB	European System of Central Banks
ESF	European Social Fund
ETSI	European Telecommunications Standard Institute
EURATOM	European Atomic Energy Community
GDP	Gross Domestic Product
GNP	Gross National Product
IMF	International Monetary Fund
MEP	Member of the European Parliament
OECD	Organization for Economic Cooperation and Development
OEEC	Organization for European Economic Cooperation
UN	United Nations
VAT	Value-Added-Tax

1

Introduction

On this shrunken globe, men can no longer live as strangers.

—Adlai E. Stevenson

Ambitions to unite the countries of Europe are not new. In the fourteenth century a Frenchman, named Pierre Dubois, proposed a European Confederation to the King of France and the Pope that was to be led by a multinational European Council. Similar notions have been suggested periodically through the years, but have always ended in failure as nations persistently sought to expand their "empires." Only the horrors of World War II, and an overwhelming desire to never repeat them, finally let cooperation prevail over aggression, enabling the foundations of what is today the European Community (EC) to be laid.

Since World War II, and certainly since the time of Dubois, the world has become a very different place. It is now smaller and more personal. Economic strength has replaced military strength as the ultimate measure of a nation, and democracy is increasingly being seen as the best solution to the difficult question of how best to govern people. Explosive growth in international trade has created a truly global economy that few could have imagined in 1945. Recent technological advances have made global communication commonplace. Information can be transmitted instantly anywhere in the world, making international business transactions both feasible and attractive. This trend is not going to reverse. Global trade will continue to grow, and as a result more and more people in the US will find themselves involved, in one way or another, with European affairs. Companies who never before considered doing business with European enterprises will begin to see the advantages, adding yet another strand to the mesh connecting the world's economies. The individual economies of the world have become so interwoven that, today, none can be said to be truly independent. This brings global sales prospects to US companies who know how to take advantage of them, but introduces increased competition that could finish those that don't.

But beyond business relationships, there are many other aspects of American life that are influenced by Europe's fortunes. Whether realized or not, the economy, stock market, currency market, monetary policies and interest rates of the US are all affected by European events. Many things commonly bought by Americans, from wine to automobiles to clothing and furniture are of European origin. Even the price of many items in the grocery store are influenced by European policies across the Atlantic.

The point of this is that European affairs *do* affect people and businesses in the United States. Even so, most Americans remain unfamiliar with the workings of the European Community—Europe's predominant political organization. Even to many of its own citizens, the intricacies of the EC bureaucracy are a bit mysterious. Yet a proper understanding of the EC should be sought by anyone wishing to succeed in the future. A future in which the idea of a global economy will accurately describe the state of the world, and a future in which the EC is sure to play an important and influential role. Knowledge of the European Community will be an indispensable asset in the future; ignorance of it could only be a detriment.

***

Although recent events have brought it increased international attention, the European Community is not a recently formed organization. Its founding treaties were signed in 1957 and were based on an even earlier organization called the European Coal and Steel Community (ECSC). The European Coal and Steel Community was formed in 1951 by six Western European nations to coordinate their coal and steel industries. From these modest beginnings, the EC has survived many growing pains to become a major force in world economics and politics. Today the EC has twelve member states (a *member state* or *member nation* being any of the countries who are members of the Community) and is involved in far more than the management of coal and steel.

Many non-EC citizens are surprised that the Community has existed for so long because they have only recently become aware of it. To a large degree, this recent fame is attributable to the extensive worldwide media coverage the Community has received in recent years due to its single European market program. This program implemented a bold plan to eliminate the Community's internal borders by the end of 1992, and the world has watched the saga with keen interest. Indeed, the preparation for the arrival of a single European market has increased global interest in the European Community, and has changed the way in which the world views Europe. No longer is Europe seen only as a conglomeration of individual nations—it is now, also, regarded as the world's largest democratic trading bloc.

The desire to eliminate borders in Europe, however, is not as modern as the media might cause one to think. The EC has attempted to minimize the importance of its internal national boundaries since the 1950s, but no previous push was ever as successful or greeted with as much enthusiasm as the recent effort. Earlier attempts to unify the European marketplace were generally either squashed from the outset by certain member nations, or accepted only with hesitancy. When progress was achieved, it was often dissolved later by protectionist legislation from the individual member states, who, for one reason or another, thought they had something to loose by encouraging free trade. In the past, the EC government was powerless when a member state passed a law that was incompatible with its policies. Often, member states took advantage of this weakness and passed laws that tended, in some way, to support their domestic interests while disregarding the desire of the Community to promote free trade. This state of affairs continued throughout the 60s and 70s simply because the political will necessary to give the EC enough authority to enforce its decisions did not exist.

Circumstances began to change, however, in the 1980s. In 1985, under a sense of renewed urgency, the member nations of the European Community began to formulate a program that would eliminate barriers to free trade. These barriers had existed in Europe for centuries, but it was finally agreed that they blocked the road toward future European prosperity and should be removed. In 1987 paperwork went into effect specifically calling for the completion of a single European market by 1992. The explicit changes necessary for the completion of the great market were spelled out in 282 directives, each one of which had to be processed through the EC's legislative system and then incorporated into every member state's national laws. The ultimate goal was to remove all existing legislation that repressed free trade—to finally make the vision of a unified European marketplace a reality.

The deadline for implementing these changes, December 31, 1992, was taken seriously. With this date now committed to history, it is possible to look at the effects of the single European market (also known as the *single market,* the *internal market,* or the *common market*) without depending so much upon conjecture. The inauguration of the single market has ushered in a new era of cooperation within Europe. Now, people, products and money are free to move about anywhere within the EC's borders with far fewer bureaucratic encumbrances than has ever before been possible. Twelve individual national markets have been effectively transformed into one enormous market with some 340 million consumers. The shear size of this market—the largest in the world—guarantees that the EC will remain an influential economic power along side the United States and Japan.

Implementing the common market is the largest, most far reaching effort that the EC has ever accomplished. Because of its expansive effects, both in Europe and globally, the press and governments around the world have heralded it as a major world political occurrence. Such status is deserved. It is one of the largest peaceful transitions of power ever accomplished in history. Its effects will not be confined just to European affairs. They will, undoubtedly, also influence the United States and the rest of the world.

But what exactly is the European Community? Why did the Single European Market finally emerge after decades of hesitancy? How does the EC operate, and what are its goals? Who are the member states of the EC, and what are their characteristics? What has been achieved and what remains to be accomplished? What makes the EC unique, and how is it able to manage its diversity (the EC has nine official languages)? These are the questions this book will answer. Its objective is to provide the reader with knowledge of the essential elements and methods of the European Community. Its intention is not to provide an in-depth technical analysis of the pros and cons of the EC, nor is it to provide specific advice to businesses as to the feasibility of seeking new markets within the EC's borders. There are other texts that grapple with these issues. This book's purpose is to provide information on the foundations from which the EC is built, and to enable the reader to gain a proper understanding of the EC's intentions and operations. It was written to familiarize the reader, in general, with the European Community, its history, its institutions and its member states so that once this groundwork is established, the reader will be better prepared to make decisions on his or her own concerning any proposed interaction with the EC. The book will provide the background necessary to enable the reader to delve more deeply into specific EC issues, and then use this information for personal benefit. Of course, even those who never interact directly with the EC will also benefit from the information in this book, if only by becoming better informed citizens of the world.

2

An Overview of the European Community

All empires, all states, all organizations of human society are, in the ultimate, things of understanding and will.

–H. G. Wells, A Short History of the World, *1929*

Due to its unique structure, the European Community defies explanation using conventional political terms. Other international organizations exist, of course, the most renowned being the United Nations. But unlike other international bodies, the EC is more than just an organization of sovereign nations. It has extensive powers of its own, and can propose and adopt legislation that is binding on its citizens and member states without additional national review or ratification. It may mandate that actions be taken by its member states to comply with EC policy, and has the power to enforce these mandates. This unique combination of characteristics gives the EC a special legal status that doesn't fit nicely into any existing category.

The primary ambitions of the EC are:

- to persuade governments to work together, both for economic reasons and to prevent war.

- to remove protectionist and bureaucratic barriers on trade.

- to reduce unemployment in its member states.

- to provide a forum that allows European nations a unified voice when negotiating agreements with the US, Japan and other outside countries.

- to encourage governments to dismantle outdated monopolies and subsidy programs.

- to confront its member states with their responsibility to the environment.

- and to make wealthier European nations recognize their responsibilities to third-world countries and the new democracies of eastern Europe.

Often, these roles make EC officials the bearer of uncomfortable truths, explaining why some Europeans resent the Community. Farmers do not enjoy seeing subsidy programs removed, and governments dislike forcing struggling industries to invest in pollution-control equipment. But the Community's importance and positive impact cannot be denied. In essence, it is a non-stop negotiating machine, bringing nations together and seeking solutions to problems that historically were "solved" by war or neglect. It is involved in many far reaching activities, and its importance as the world's largest trading bloc makes its decisions felt worldwide.

It is tempting to view the EC as a federation. A federation is loosely defined as an organization whose members have agreed to entrust common affairs to a central authority. In the normal, political sense of the term, the affairs controlled by the central authority (the federal government) consist of at least foreign and monetary policy. Though the EC has many supranational powers, it is not a true federation. A true federation, such as the United States or Germany, is able to speak to the world with a common voice regarding certain political matters. The state of Nebraska, for example, cannot independently announce that it has declared war on Iraq. A decision of this importance must be made at the federal level by the United States government. In the United States, each of the 50 states are subordinate to the Federal government in many areas, including foreign and monetary policy. In the EC system, the member states individually retain their nationhood—they are not sub-national entities. Spain, Germany, or any other member nation of the EC could declare war independently on another nation if it so desired. The member nations of the EC do, however, relinquish control of some of their affairs, and they grant the institutions of the European Community the ability and authority to coordinate Community-wide policies in some areas. By coordinating these policies, the government of the EC tries to promote growth and international cooperation, and to avoid the market protectionism, stagnation and war that has occurred historically in Europe.

Since its creation—a spectacular achievement in itself—the most outstanding accomplishment of the Community has been the establishment of the single European market. Work began on the program in 1985 under legislation called the Single European Act. The Single European Act empowered a plan to systematically remove trade barriers between the EC's member nations. Its four fundamental goals—the free movement of goods, people, services and money—were to be accomplished by December 31, 1992. The deadline was largely met. All of the necessary proposals were written and approved by the EC well ahead of the 1992 deadline so that the member states would have time to adopt them into their national laws. Since 1985, the member nations have embraced most of the reforms and the transformation has brought a new face to Europe. For both EC citizens and others, Europe now offers many new and exciting opportunities.

What has the 1992 single-market program accomplished?

The best way to convey the significance and breadth of the single-market program is through some specific, hypothetical examples. The following acts were not possible before the single-market program due to protectionist laws and differing standards. Now they are. The unveiling of the Single Market allows:

- a German doctor to practice medicine in Brussels, or any other city within the EC.

- an American or Japanese citizen to enter the EC in any country, pass through customs once, and then travel throughout the twelve nations of the Community without ever being stopped by another immigration or customs official.

- EC corporations from different countries to merge with one another.

- an EC citizen to search for a job anywhere within the EC.

- a truck traveling from Spain to Denmark to make the journey without the hassle of multiple customs checks and border delays, making the time and cost of the journey significantly less.

Further, the Single Market allows:

- a European family to relocate itself from Germany to Belgium as easily as an American family can move from Colorado to Utah (in terms of bureaucratic hassles).

- a car manufactured in Germany to be subject to the same pollution-control laws as a car manufactured in Spain.

- EC citizens to use their national/EC passports to obtain assistance at the embassies and consulates of any EC country, anywhere in the world.

- EC students to earn a degree at any accredited institution within the EC's borders, and know it will be recognized throughout the Community.

The Institutions of the EC—an Introduction

As is the case with most complex organizations, the European Community, taken as a whole, is far more than the sum of its parts. The raw building blocks from which the EC draws life are its institutions. Four fundamental institutions comprise the political structure of the EC.

The primary operating body is called the Commission. It consists of 17 members (Commissioners) who are collectively appointed by the member states, but are sworn to serve the interests of the Community and may "neither seek nor take instructions from any government or any body."[1] The Commission represents the voice of the Community as a whole. It is interested in the concerns of the EC—not in those of the individual member nations. The concerns of the individual member states are introduced into the EC's system through the Council of Ministers. The Council is composed of twelve national ministers, each representing a member government. The other primary institutions are the European Parliament and the Court of Justice. The European Parliament consists of 518 members who are directly elected by European citizens and, thereby, most dependably represent their views.

---

1. *Treaty Establishing the European Economic Community* (Rome: March 25, 1957).

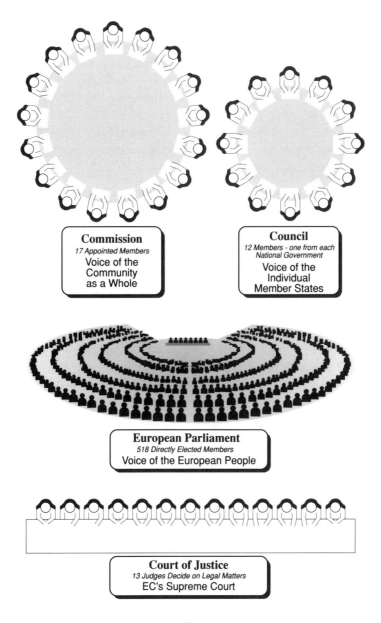

Commission
17 Appointed Members
Voice of the
Community
as a Whole

Council
12 Members - one from each
National Government
Voice of the
Individual
Member States

European Parliament
518 Directly Elected Members
Voice of the European People

Court of Justice
13 Judges Decide on Legal Matters
EC's Supreme Court

The European Community's Four Primary Institutions

The Court of Justice serves as the Community's Supreme Court, making judgments on questions of legality and interpretation. The figure on the preceding page provides a simple graphic representation of the EC's four main institutions. Though the roles attributed to each institution are highly generalized, the figure serves as a necessary introduction, illustrating the fundamental differences between the Community's institutions.

The EC's institutions will be examined more thoroughly in Chapter 4, following a succinct chronology of the Community's development.

What the EC is not—dispelling some misconceptions

There are some misunderstandings about the EC that need to be clarified. A common, wrongly-held, belief is that the EC's single-market program was put in place for the benefit of its consumers. This is not true. Although some EC propaganda would tend to suggest otherwise, the single-market program was not a consumer movement. The broad reforms were not undertaken simply to provide more choice and better prices for consumers, although these are welcome by-products of the transformation. Nor, can the single market be said to have been caused by a renaissance of laissez-faire capitalism in Europe. In reality, the single-market program was accomplished for political reasons that arose when Europe found itself falling economically behind the United States and Japan. The economic problems of the individual nations were of such similar nature that a pan-European effort provided each nation with a better solution than it could hope to achieve on its own. Finding themselves in similar circumstances, the nations of the EC joined together to create a common market. This unity enabled the approval of the single-market program's various initiatives—changes that previously would have certainly been rejected. Detailed reasons for the establishment of the single market will be discussed in Chapter 5.

Next, to avoid confusion, some clarification in terminology regarding the name *European Community* is required. For many years the "European Community," or "EC," was more commonly known as the EEC—the European Economic Community. Some texts speak of the European *Communities*, which is, strictly speaking, proper. These variances, and the confusion caused by them, have come about because the "European Community" is in actuality, and by law, a conglomeration of *three* communities: the European Coal and Steel Community (ECSC), the European Economic Community (EEC) and the European Atomic Energy Community (Euratom). Due to the gymnastics of tongue required to recite this lengthy sequence of titles, the term "European Community" has evolved to include (unofficially) all three communities. Furthermore, the Single European Act and the arrival of the common market are often referred to as having been created by the "European Community." Actually, the common market was enacted by the European *Economic* Community, but this distinction is generally not important. Officially, the term "Economic" in EEC exists because the EEC was created primarily to promote economic integration between its member states. The EC nomenclature is intended to represent, much to the satisfaction of many "pro-Europe" advocates, a European union not only in economic terms, but also in terms of political, fiscal and social aspects. An *official* name change will occur if present efforts to politically integrate the European Community are successful.

Despite US opinions to the contrary, the EC is not the "United States of Europe." This is true for many reasons including the absence of a common currency and lack of a single foreign policy. Still, similarities can be observed between the vast free marketplace in the United States and the EC's common market. There certainly is a faction within the EC's bureaucracy that would indeed like to create a true, "US-style" federation in Europe, thereby rendering the name the "United States of Europe" accurate. This, however, is presently not the case. Many Europeans are offended by the thought of a "United States of Europe," as it implies that their individual nationality and their nation's sovereignty would be, to them, unacceptably reduced. A Danish man publicly said that he didn't want Denmark to become "the Minnesota of Europe." The degree of federalization, i.e., the amount of central control that the EC should adopt, is now, and has historically been, one of the Community's most hotly debated topics.

Another feature of the EC, which is often misunderstood, is the way it interacts with national citizenship. The single market has enabled EC citizens to function as "Europeans" (as opposed to, say, Germans or Italians) both commercially and professionally. This is comparable to the situation in the US where US citizens function as "Americans," as opposed to Texans or Californians, in many circumstances. This means, an EC lawyer may practice law anywhere in the Community, and EC citizens can establish a bank account in any member state, just as in the US. But in the EC, these new abilities do not extend to political activity, revealing an important distinction between the United States and the European Community.

To illustrate this, consider the following: the EC's single market has made it possible for a German to practice his profession and live in France, yet he must return to Germany to vote, get a divorce, or complete any other action of a political nature. In the United States, if people move from state to state, their political rights follow them. A US citizen may vote in Presidential elections from whichever state they are residing. In the EC, the president and members of the Commission (the chief operating body of the EC) are not elected officials. Only the members of the European Parliament are elected by "Europeans," but the role of the European Parliament (discussed in Chapter 4) seems destined to remain second to that of the member state's national parliaments. So, although the German professional living in France may vote for a member of the European Parliament while in France, the more meaningful ballot must be cast in Germany when voting for the members of the Bundestag (lower house of the German Parliament). The single market program does not make any provisions for the German professional to vote in the French national elections, even though it does allow him to live and work there (current efforts wish to change this situation through an EC common citizenship).

Misunderstanding also revolves around the actual significance of the December 31, 1992, deadline for implementing the single-market reforms. The media covered the event in such a way that it was given an almost magical significance—as if the European economic pumpkin would transform overnight into a shimmering example of democratic market perfection at the end of 1992. The deadline, however, was not so magical and did not represent the end of the European integration process. Rather, it signified the beginning of a new era of economic cooperation in Europe. The deadline marked the completion of the first step—the fulfillment of the measures necessary to get the common market rolling. It signifies the beginning, not the end, of the Community's integration efforts. Legislation, that will further harmonize the EC's operations, will continue to be proposed, negotiated and eventually passed into law. The European marketplace is not finished now that 1992 has past—it will evolve for many years, even decades to come.

Finally, certain limitations of the Single European Market must be kept in mind when discussing the EC, particularly when attempting to compare it to the US market. Although the common market does make it possible for an unemployed Irish machinist to go to France and get a job with a French company, in most cases it is unlikely that he would choose to do so because it would imply moving to a country that, although certainly to a lesser degree than 100 years ago, is still quite foreign. The prospect of raising his family in such an alien environment is not likely to be very appealing, and all other alternatives in Ireland and then in England will no doubt be explored first. Europe is a very diverse continent, and regardless of the bureaucratic possibility of such moves, moving from Portugal to the Netherlands is simply not the same as moving from Utah to Wyoming.

3

The History of the European Community

You cannot divide peace in Europe. You must have one peace running right through.

–Clement Attlee, British Politician, 1936

Discontent is the first step in the progress of a man or a nation.

—Oscar Wilde, A Woman of No Importance, *1893*

Membership in the EC has doubled since the six original nations organized themselves in 1951. Its institutions have grown and become more complex, and several new treaties have been signed, each giving the Community additional powers and responsibilities. A historical examination of these developments provides a good foundation from which to build an understanding of the Community, its purpose, its origins and its destination. This chapter presents the history of the EC without unnecessary elaboration or complication. From it, the reader will gain an understanding of the spirit in which, and reasons for which, the Community was created. It provides the necessary background to investigate what is happening today in Europe, and is a useful overview for later, more in-depth, specific inquiries. For easy reference, a concise chronological summary of dates and events that are significant to the evolution of the European Community can be found at the back of this book.

The First 20 Years

1951—The Establishment of the European Coal and Steel Community

The history of Europe, for essentially as long as history has been recorded, has been a succession of wars and of drives toward empire. The wake of World War II left Europe horribly battered, and created a desire to seek greater cooperation between the countries of Europe in order to avoid such pointless destruction and violence from ever repeating itself. Toward this end, Germany and France agreed to form a coalition to pool and centrally manage their production of coal and steel—these being the fundamental fuels of a war machine. Robert Schuman, the French minister of foreign affairs, formally proposed such an arrangement in September 1950. The arrangement was to be open to all European countries, but was agreed upon initially by Germany and France, who intended to go ahead with the plan with or without the participation of other nations. This proposal, known as the Schuman Declaration, led to the formation of the European Coal and Steel Community (ECSC), which is the basis and birthplace of today's European Community. Other nations did accept the invitation to participate, and on April 18, 1951, the *Treaty Establishing the European Coal and Steel Community* was signed in Paris by Germany, France, Belgium, Italy, Luxembourg and the Netherlands. This treaty has become commonly known as either the *Treaty of Paris,* or the *ECSC Treaty.* The six countries who signed it are known as "The Six." They are the original member nations of what is today the European Community. The European Coal and Steel Community established four decision-making bodies: the High Authority, the Council of Ministers, the Court of Justice, and the Parliamentary Assembly. These institutions formed the foundation from which the institutional structure of the modern European Community was built.

Shortly after the European Coal and Steel Community was founded, tensions between the United States and the Soviet Union lead to the idea of the European Defense Community (EDC). It has been said that the best way to promote union among Europeans is through a common enemy, and the threat of an East-West conflict, potentially centered in Europe, worried European leaders. They recognized that the best way to form a viable defense for their homelands was through the association and pooling of European resources. The EDC was designed to do this. Its purpose was to coordinate the armed forces of Europe, essentially creating a European army. A second organization, the European Political Community (EPC), was also proposed to complement the military union through political cooperation.

The European Defense Community Treaty contained ideas that would have produced enormous steps toward integrating Europe. It envisioned an eventual merger between the ECSC, the EDC and the EPC to create a new organization with a parliament, a council of ministers, and a court of justice (not coincidentally three of the four institutions of today's EC). But the ambitions of the EDC Treaty never materialized. It was accepted by five of the six national parliaments; but France, the founder of the idea, was unable to muster the required support from its National Assembly and the treaty had to be abandoned. The reservations held by those opposed to the EDC Treaty were diverse. Some of the fundamental concerns were: uneasiness about rearming Germany, hesitation to relinquish sole control of national military forces, apprehension caused by the United Kingdom's lack of participation, and doubts about the efficiency of a common "European army."

The failure of the European Defense Community revealed that in spite of political talk to the contrary, the leaders of Europe were dedicated foremost to the prosperity of their own countries. If circumstances seemed to mandate such action, policies would be chosen based on domestic preference regardless of whether they were beneficial to the cause of European unity. Further, it showed that if European integration was to occur, it would have to be achieved by way of a succession of small steps instituted by treaties dealing with specific attributes of integration, rather than by one grandiose, all encompassing treaty. The Treaty of Rome, the founding document of the European Economic Community, would later reflect this more refined and practical thinking.

Although the EDC failed, it made far more progress than would have been possible a decade earlier, and showed that alternative initiatives might be successful. In June 1955, the Foreign Ministers of the ECSC's six member nations met in Messina, Italy in hopes of specifying other ways to integrate Europe. Knowing that the military union, proposed by the European Defense Community, had failed, a union based on economic terms was suggested instead. An intergovernmental committee was formed under the leadership of Belgian Foreign Minister Paul-Henri Spaak. The Spaak committee explored creating an organization similar to the ECSC to centrally manage nuclear energy development, and examined ways to expand the economic ties between the six member states. Its report was subsequently approved by all six member states, and would be used later to negotiate the treaties for the European Atomic Energy Community and the European Economic Community.

1957—The Treaty of Rome, the European Economic Community and Euratom

Following the meetings in Messina, the "Six" gathered again, this time in Rome, to agree upon specific treaties based on the principals of the Spaak Report. On March 25, 1957, representatives of the Six signed two treaties—one establishing the European Economic Community, and the other establishing the European Atomic Energy Community (Euratom). Though two separate treaties were actually signed in Rome, today they are often bundled together and referred to singularly as the *Treaty of Rome.*

These treaties established many new institutions. The EEC and Euratom were both given their own Council and Commission. The Parliamentary Assembly and Court of Justice, formerly established by the ECSC, were modified, becoming joint institutions shared by all three Communities.

The preamble to the Treaty of Rome was written with powerful words describing its purpose as being, "to lay the foundations of an ever-closer union among the peoples of Europe...and by common action to *eliminate the barriers* which divide Europe."[2] This statement shows that, even as early as 1957, the elimination of borders, i.e., the establishment of a single market, was a primary goal. The treaty's founding fathers hoped that the organization created by the treaty would evolve into something more than simply an economic association of six countries. Many hoped that the EEC would be the first major step in the process initiated by the Treaty of Paris toward fulfilling a vision of a united Europe—a Europe united not only economically, but socially and politically as well. In view of these long term aspirations, clauses were included in the Treaty of Rome that would allow the possibility of eventually coordinating social and political policies, though no specific plans were spelled out.

The Treaty expressed hope that the elimination of barriers within the EC would serve as a catalyst toward achieving "continuous and balanced expansion, an increase in stability, an accelerated raising of the standard of living and closer relations between the States belonging to it." In the late 1950s, after expe-

---

2. *Treaty Establishing the European Economic Community* (Rome: March 25, 1957).

riencing the emotional and economic ravages of World War II, many people in Europe felt that prosperity could only be developed through international cooperation.

With these lofty ambitions as long term goals, the immediate objectives of the European Economic Community were:

- to provide uniform customs duties for goods that entered any member state from outside the Community,

- to eliminate quota restrictions, customs duties, and equivalent taxes on inter-EEC, cross-border goods,

- to abolish restrictions on the free movement of community citizens, services and capital,

- to permit any firm to operate in any member state in the community, subject to equivalent laws and taxes,

- to prevent governments from giving advantages to their home businesses over and above the advantages given to non-home country businesses and,

- to establish common transport and agricultural policies.[3]

As will be seen, some of these goals were successfully accomplished, others were only partly accomplished, and still others were initially achieved, yet later nullified by national laws. Only recently have these goals been honestly obtained.

1960—EFTA founded

Not every nation in Europe was enthusiastic about the far reaching ideals expressed in the Treaty of Rome. It is important to note that the United Kingdom, one of the strongest and most influential countries in Europe during the 1950s, was not a member of the original Six, nor was it one of the signatories of the Treaty of Rome. This is certainly not because the UK was unwelcome. It could have signed the Treaty of Paris, and was invited to the Messina conferences where the Treaty of Rome was conceived. In fact, the UK did participate in the first five months of the

---

3. *Treaty Establishing the European Economic Community* (Rome: March 25, 1957).

Messina conferences, and spent the entire time trying to limit the scope of the organization under discussion. It wanted the new organization to be nothing more than an economic free trade area—not the broader organization with social and political aspects that was sanctioned by the Six. When it became obvious that the UK's efforts were to be unsuccessful, it withdrew from the proceedings in Messina.

Other important Western European nations, too, did not participate in the Messina conferences. Their absence indicated that they were not comfortable with the high level of association desired by the Six. Indeed, for various reasons many Western European nations were not ready to accept the high degree of association implied by the Treaty of Rome and thus, opted to remain outside the EEC. Though not wanting to join the EEC, most of these nations felt economically insecure remaining alone outside of it.

A common point of view among the divergent nations was that a more narrowly defined organization, one based solely on economic association, would better suit their interests than the broader organization proposed by the Six. These common ideas and concerns led to a meeting of representatives from the United Kingdom, Denmark, Austria, Sweden, Switzerland, Norway and Portugal on May 3, 1960 in Stockholm, Sweden. There, a different kind of international European organization was created—the European Free Trade Association (EFTA). As the name implies, EFTA seeks free trade in industrial goods between its member states, and encourages participation in world trade outside its borders. Unlike the EEC's Treaty of Rome, which endorses political and social union, EFTA's founding documents contain no suggestions of international cooperation beyond economic accords.

EFTA has played an important indirect role in the EC's maturation and is the EC's primary trading partner. Today EFTA consists of Austria, Iceland, Norway, Sweden, Switzerland, Finland and Liechtenstein. Every EFTA member nation except Iceland and Liechtenstein have applied for membership with the EC. An agreement has been made forming an EC-EFTA European Economic Area (EEA) through which many of the benefits of the EC's single market will be extended to the EFTA countries. A more thorough discussion of EFTA and the European Economic Area will be postponed until Chapter 8.

1962—The Common Agricultural Policy

In the early 1960s surging international competition helped EC member nations realize the benefit of their alliance, and the Community's responsibilities began to grow. One of the more important EC policies, the Common Agricultural Policy (CAP), was born in 1962. The Common Agricultural Policy was established to maintain common prices for agricultural products throughout the Community, and to stabilize farm incomes by guaranteeing minimum prices through farm subsidies. The funds for these subsidies have become the Community's largest expense, making up 64% of the EC's budget in 1990. Today contention exists between the EC Commission, who would like to limit the Community's agricultural expenditures, and the ministers in the Council, who are under national political pressures to maintain them.

1967—The Merger Treaty

Before 1967, the ECSC, the EEC and Euratom were distinct organizations. Though they had shared a common Court of Justice and Parliament since 1958, each had a distinct Council and executive Commission (called the "High Authority" in the ECSC). In 1967, the three Communities merged their executive and decision-making bodies to form, in essence, a single European Community. This merger was accomplished through a treaty signed in Brussels in 1965 that replaced the three separate Councils and Commissions with a single Council and a single Commission, as depicted graphically in the figure on the next page. The new Council and new Commission assumed all the powers and responsibilities previously held by their predecessors, while the European Parliament and the Court of Justice remained common to the three communities as they had been since 1958. The institutional structure that resulted from the merger treaty remains essentially unchanged today.

Though the three European Communities are now managed by common institutions, the powers exercised by the merged institutions are still based on the individual founding treaties; that is to say that the treaties and the Communities themselves were not merged—only the institutions were. Thus, a Community ruling regarding the steel industry is arrived at and enforced through the provisions of the Treaty of Paris (ECSC Treaty), and a ruling

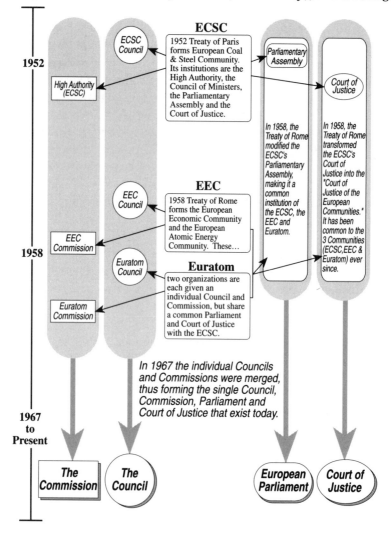

**The Merger Treaty and the Evolution
of the EC's Present Institutions**

regarding the single European market falls under the jurisdiction of the Treaty of Rome (Treaty Establishing the EEC). Since the different treaties have varying definitions of the laws enacted under them, a Council *Decision* under the ECSC treaty is a much stronger piece of legislation than a Council *Decision* under the Treaty of Rome. The various types of legislation that result from the different definitions in the treaties will be discussed in the next chapter.

1968—Internal duties eliminated

In 1968 the EEC established a Customs Union between its six member nations, achieving the free movement of goods sought after by the Treaty of Rome. The Customs Union eliminated duties between EEC countries, and set a common external tariff for goods coming from outside the EEC (replacing the individual national tariffs that were previously in place). The implementation of the Customs Union was a strong step toward realizing the common-market goals of the Treaty of Rome, but it only affected the distribution of goods. Measures that permitted the uninhibited movement of people, services, and capital remained unfulfilled goals.

The Expansion of the EC

Today, the European Community embraces over 340 million people—twice as many as there were when the original Six signed the Treaty of Rome in 1952. This expansion has radically altered the external borders of the Community, adding six new member nations to the original six. The Community's role in world affairs has been strengthened with each new member state, and each expansion has enriched the Community culturally. As shown in the figure on the following page, the Community's growth has occurred in three phases. In 1973, Denmark, Ireland and the UK joined the EC; they were followed by Greece (1981), and Spain and Portugal in 1986. The accession of these nations was the result of years of intense and often difficult negotiations. The essence of the story, though, can be told succinctly.

In 1962, only two years after the formation of EFTA, the United Kingdom had a change of heart and decided to apply for EC membership. The reasons for the change of stance were both economic and political. Economically, the member states of the EC were outperforming the United Kingdom in all the usual measures. This convinced UK officials that EC membership would probably help the troubled British economy. Politically, world events were increasingly showing that the UK was no longer the indomitable

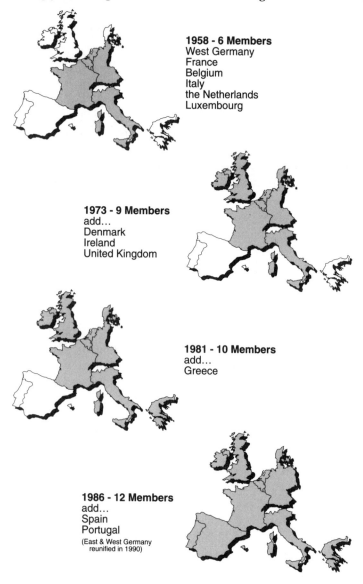

1958 - 6 Members
West Germany
France
Belgium
Italy
the Netherlands
Luxembourg

1973 - 9 Members
add...
Denmark
Ireland
United Kingdom

1981 - 10 Members
add...
Greece

1986 - 12 Members
add...
Spain
Portugal
(East & West Germany
   reunified in 1990)

world leader that it once was. The EC appeared to be linked with a growing political status and it was thought that membership might increase the UK's sagging political stance.

Britain, thus, became convinced that the Community was a desirable club to belong to. But despite its heavily soul-searched decision, the UK's application was rejected. The dismissal was mostly due to the complaints of France's president, Charles de Gaulle, whose objections were cloaked in a thinly disguised veil asserting that the original six should more thoroughly complete the initial stages of economic consolidation before allowing other nations to become members. In reality, De Gaulle's objections were based on fear that Britain would remove France from its position of dominance within the EC.

Not to be disenchanted by the initial rejection, the United Kingdom reapplied for Community membership in 1970. This time President de Gaulle (of France) was no longer in office, and no objection was made. Applications for membership were also accepted from Norway, Denmark and Ireland, who applied simultaneously with the UK due to traditional economic and cultural links with it. In 1973, after extensive negotiations, the United Kingdom, Denmark and Ireland were allowed admission into the EC. Much to the regret of the Norwegian government, Norway was forced to remove its application from consideration due to a referendum that resulted in 53% of the voting population casting votes against Norway's EC membership.

In 1981, Greece was allowed membership in the Community bringing the total number of member nations in the EC to 10. The membership of Greece had been delayed for many years due to the underdeveloped nature of the Greek economy. When Greece first applied for membership shortly after the EEC was established, Community officials deemed that a transition period was necessary and Greece was given "Associate" status in 1962. The purpose of the Associate status was to give Greece time to spruce up its economy; full membership was to be granted once Greece was capable of sustaining the obligations imposed by membership in the Community. The Association Agreement was, however, effectively suspended from April 1967 until June 1974 due to a military coup in Greece. When a civilian government was again established in 1974, the Commission issued a formal Opinion stating that Greece was still not economically ready to join the EC and that a transition period of unlimited duration, during which economic reforms were implemented, was required.

The Greek government responded by restating its desire for full membership and further supported their argument by saying that membership in the EC would help to firmly establish Greek democracy. This was seen as an important argument in view of Greece's recent struggle with dictatorship during its 1967-1974 military coup. Furthermore, events that took place during the coup nearly led Greece into a war with Turkey. Such a war was a hazard that every official in the EC wanted to avoid. Admitting Greece into the Community was considered a way to greatly diminish the possibility of any future Greek-Turk confrontation. In view of these arguments, the Council of Ministers agreed with the Greek's plea for full EC membership and negotiations began in 1976 leading to the 1981 accession of Greece.

The 1986 accession of Portugal and Spain brought the total number of EC member states to twelve, where it remains today. Both Spain and Portugal had applied for EC membership as early as 1962, but the political situation then made acceptance unfeasible. The Community viewed the applications with caution primarily due to dictatorial governments that existed then in both Spain and Portugal. Preferential trading agreements were established with Spain in 1970 and with Portugal in 1973, but serious consideration for EC membership was not possible until after the fall of the reigning dictatorships. In 1975, Spain's ruler, General Franco, died ending his rule of nearly four decades. One year earlier, in 1974, the existing repressive regime in Portugal was overthrown. With the dictatorships gone, serious negotiations toward Portuguese and Spanish EC membership were finally able to begin. The negotiations took eight years, but ultimately led to the 1986 accession of Spain and Portugal—proudly making them the most recent nations to join the Community.

Eurosclerosis

The period between 1973 and 1984 marked a definite slow-down in the Community's integration efforts—it is often referred to as the period of "Eurosclerosis." Though the Community did add six new member states and introduce some important legislation during those years, overall the Community stagnated in the 1970s and early 1980s. National legislators began to pass protectionist laws which effectively replaced the tariffs that had been removed by the Customs Union in 1967. There was continual intra-country bickering—the UK complained about the EC budget, Germany urged the adoption of economic policies similar to its own, France scrambled to regain its position of dominance in EC affairs, and everyone griped about agricultural subsidies, quotas and product design standards.

The lack of common ambitions that led to these arguments was caused primarily by the world recession. Many member states resorted to protectionist measures when their economies began to sour and cooperation within the Community's institutions suffered. But when the US and Japanese economies recovered, most European economies remained depressed. The protectionist policies, which European nations had relied on for decades to keep their industries healthy, had become ineffective. Only after this was recognized, and politicians understood the economic necessity of European cooperation, was the EC able to resume its drive for greater European union.

Since 1985—The Single Market and the Treaty of Maastricht

"Eurosclerosis" was finally squashed by the single-market program. Its accomplishments, which are detailed in a later chapter, breathed new life into the EC and paved the way for further unification efforts.

In November 1991, a European Summit was held in Maastricht, Netherlands, where European leaders drafted a new treaty that they hoped would allow the Community to become even more integrated, both politically and economically. The treaty has not yet been ratified, but, if adopted, it would create a common currency, foster a common foreign policy and promote a joint defense policy.

Also, the name, "European Community," would be officially adopted (rather than European Economic Community) and the Community's citizens would be given common citizenship allowing them to vote and run in municipal elections regardless of where they live and work. As will be revealed in later discussions, the Maastricht Treaty is far from uncontroversial. Debate rages over its pros and cons, but all the while it serves as a necessary focal point, enabling the Community's integration efforts to proceed.

The EC's "Constitution"

By 1958, the six original members of the ECSC had subscribed to a total of three treaties: the Treaty of Paris, The Treaty of Rome establishing the EEC, and the Treaty of Rome establishing Euratom. These three documents, taken together, may be thought of as the "Constitution of the European Community" and compared to the Constitution of the United States or to those of other nations. The fundamental difference between the "Constitution of the EC" and those of most sovereign nations is that it has specific matters of policy as its primary concern (for example, the policy of establishing the single market). In contrast, national constitutions generally say very little about *specific policy* matters, devoting their pages to *principals* of public policy. The important thing, though, is simply to recognize that the three above mentioned treaties are the documents that form the fundamental legal basis from which the European Community operates. As will be discussed later, the treaties have been augmented and amended through the years, but the basic legal framework that they provide was put in place 35 years ago.

Summary

The history of the Community can be succinctly expressed by examining the various treaties that have established and shaped it through the years. The following table does just that. The story can be recounted as follows:

Today's EC began when the European Coal and Steel Community was founded in 1951. It evolved further in 1957 through the creation of the European Economic Community and the European Atomic Energy Community. In 1967, the Merger Treaty simplified matters by combining the institutions of the three, formerly individual communities, creating the single European Community spoken of today. Since that time, there has been three periods of expansion, doubling the number of EC countries from its original six to its present twelve. In 1987, the Single European Act came into force, beginning the countdown toward the 1992 single European market, which officially opened on January 1, 1993. Currently, the EC's focus is on the Treaty of Maastricht which, if adopted, will increase the Community's level of economic and political integration, and set the tone for the next decade.

Treaty	Date and Place Signed	Date Treaty Came Into Force
European Coal and Steel Community (ECSC)	April 18, 1951 Paris, France	July 23, 1952
European Economic Community (EEC) & European Atomic Energy Community (Euratom)	March 25, 1957 Rome, Italy	January 1, 1958
Merger Treaty (merged the ECSC, the EEC and Euratom. Created a single Council and a single Commission)	April 8, 1965 Rome, Italy	July 1, 1967
Entry of Denmark, Ireland and the United Kingdom into the Community	January 2, 1972 Brussels, Belgium	January 1, 1973
Entry of Greece into the Community	May 28, 1979 Athens, Greece	January 1, 1981
Entry of Spain and Portugal into the Community	June 12, 1985 Madrid, Spain & Lisbon, Portugal	January 1, 1986
Single European Act (signed in two sessions)	February 17, 1986 Luxembourg & February 28, 1986 The Hague, Netherlands	July 1, 1987
Treaty on European Union (The Maastricht Treaty)	December, 1991 Maastricht, Netherlands	Not Yet Ratified

4

The Institutions and Legislative Process of the European Community

Social advance depends as much upon the process through which it is secured as upon the result itself.

— Jane Addams

As previously mentioned, the European Community's extensive legislative powers distinguish it from other international organizations. Its ability to create laws that promote the common interest of the entire Community and then impose them on the member states is an arrangement that is unmatched anywhere else. The procedures that are responsible for developing these laws face a delicate task—getting twelve nations, often with widely varying interests, to agree on the content of EC rules. Though it is not perfect, the Community's legislative system has generally proven itself capable of this challenge.

As we have seen, the Community has four primary institutions. The *Council* makes final decisions on whether proposals become law or not. The *Commission* drafts new proposals and implements approved proposals. The *European Parliament* delivers opinions on the various proposals, and the *Court of Justice* serves as the Community's "Supreme Court," enforcing community law and making interpretations when necessary.

Additionally, two ancillary organizations also play important parts in the Community's decision making process. The *Economic and Social Committee* serves as a consultative body with 189 members representing trade unions, employers and various other special interest groups such as farmers and consumers; and, the *Court of Auditors* acts as the Community's accountant. Its twelve members are responsible for auditing all the Community's financial activities and providing opinions regarding the economic consequences of various proposals.

The interaction between these institutions is the lifeblood of the EC. From it emerges the laws upon which the Community is built. The procedures that guide this interaction cause an interplay of forces designed to avoid alienation or domination by any one interest—a key objective of the Community's founding treaties. Though the process creates laws that the member states must comply with, it is not like that of a true federation. It is a unique arrangement—one that is perhaps best described as a "Community" system.

A basic description of the interactions that take place between the institutions is shown in the figure below. The figure divides the legislative process into three phases: Drafting the proposal, Debating its contents, and Enactment.

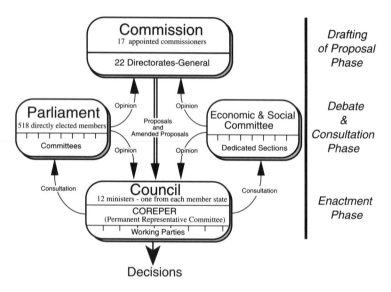

Interaction between the EC's Institutions

As shown by the figure, a large amount of consultation and opinion taking occurs between the institutions during the legislative process. These interactions occur through two primary legislative processes, but before the processes can be explained, a discussion of what a "law" is in the Community is necessary.

The Community's "Laws"—Directives, Decisions, etc.

The EC's legislative process results in completed legal instruments that are not, strictly speaking, called "laws." Rather, they are termed *Regulations, Directives, Decisions, Recommendations* or *Opinions,* depending upon the amount of authority they carry, and whether the Council is acting under the Treaty of Paris

(EEC treaty) or the Treaty of Rome (ECSC and Euratom treaties). Under the Treaty of Rome, which applies to all EEC legislation including proposals related to the single-market program, the various types of legislation are defined as follows:

- Regulations are very general and are directly applicable in all member states; they are comparable to national laws.

- Directives lay down compulsory objectives, but leave it to the member states to transpose them into their national legislation.

- Decisions are binding only on specifically addressed parties, i.e., member states, firms or specific individuals.

- Recommendations and Opinions, are not binding but are given as guidance. [4]

Since the majority of the Community's activities fall under the direction of the Treaty of Rome, most EC laws are one of the above four types. But when acting on matters concerning the European Coal and Steel Community, under the Treaty of Paris, only three types of legislation are issued.

- Decisions are the strongest type of legislation, and are binding in their entirety.

- Recommendations are essentially the same as Directives under the Treaty of Rome as outlined above.

- Opinions are non-binding advice, just as they are under the Treaty of Rome.

Thus, a "Decision" issued under the authority of the ECSC is a much more powerful piece of legislation than a "Decision" concerning the single market or any other area under the jurisdiction of the Treaty of Rome. The relationship between the various types of legislation, produced by the EC, can be confusing. It is, perhaps, best explained by the figure on the next page.

---

4. European File Series, 1991, *The Institutions of the EC*, Luxembourg: Office of the Official Publications of the European Communities.

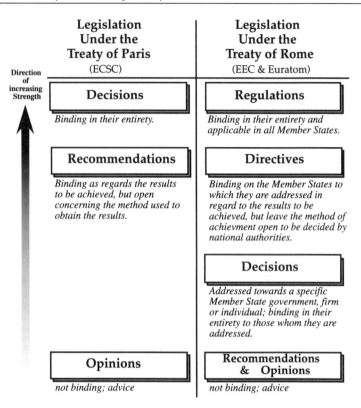

Legislation Under the Treaty of Paris (ECSC)	Legislation Under the Treaty of Rome (EEC & Euratom)
Decisions	**Regulations**
Binding in their entirety.	*Binding in their entirety and applicable in all Member States.*
Recommendations	**Directives**
Binding as regards the results to be achieved, but open concerning the method used to obtain the results.	*Binding on the Member States to which they are addressed in regard to the results to be achieved, but leave the method of achievment open to be decided by national authorities.*
	Decisions
	Addressed towards a specific Member State government, firm or individual; binding in their entirety to those whom they are addressed.
Opinions	**Recommendations & Opinions**
not binding; advice	*not binding; advice*

Direction of increasing Strength

*The Various Types of Legislation
produced by the EC Legislative System*

The EC's Legislative Processes

Before 1987, the Community used essentially one process to pass all new legislation. The process, called the "consultation procedure" or the "single-reading procedure," is depicted in the figure on the next page. Essentially, the procedure works as follows: The Commission, with the opinion of the Parliament, and the Economic and Social Committee drafts a new proposal and submits it to the Council for approval. The Council may then make one of three choices: it may approve the proposal as written, amend it if a unanimous amendment can be agreed upon, or reject it. From 1958 to 1965 the Treaty of Rome required that Council decisions be unanimous. After 1966, the treaty envisioned that most decisions would be made by majority vote. But disagreements regarding majority voting followed, and the Council ministers usually sought unanimity anyway—even when not strictly necessary. This tended to drastically slow the adoption of new laws.

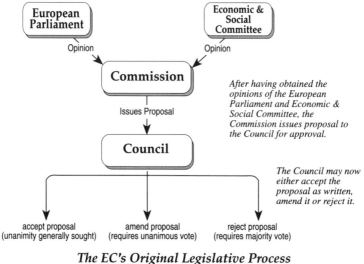

European Parliament

Economic & Social Committee

Opinion   Opinion

Commission

Issues Proposal

After having obtained the opinions of the European Parliament and Economic & Social Committee, the Commission issues proposal to the Council for approval.

Council

The Council may now either accept the proposal as written, amend it or reject it.

accept proposal
(unanimity generally sought)

amend proposal
(requires unanimous vote)

reject proposal
(requires majority vote)

*The EC's Original Legislative Process
—the "Consultation Procedure"*

The dramatic changes that occurred during the 1980s made it apparent that some improvements were needed in the way legislation was adopted. When the single-market program was introduced in 1985, the sluggishness of the Council was seen as a potential threat to its success. Additionally, the European Parliament, which had long been dissatisfied with its limited role in the legislative process, became particularly ardent in its pleas for more influence.

The Single European Act introduced two significant measures toward alleviating these concerns. First, the Act made qualified majority voting (a weighted voting system described later that requires 54 of 76 votes for approval) the standard for any Council decision involving the single market, thus speeding up the decision-making process. Second, a new legislative procedure was introduced that supplemented the original "consultation procedure" by increasing the Parliament's role in the process.

The new procedure, which is generally known as the "cooperation procedure," is applicable to all qualified majority decisions that concern the single market, economic and social cohesion, social policy or research. It was used for virtually all the proposals necessary for the single-market program, and has thus been highly practiced. Under the new procedure, the European Parliament attains closer liaison with both the Commission and the Council through first and second readings of all proposals as they pass through the adoption process. The details of the "cooperation procedure" are provided by the figure on the next page.

A Closer Look at the Primary Institutions

The Council of Ministers and European Council

Unlike the members of the EC's other institutions, the twelve ministers of the Council are not permanent representatives—the ministers change depending on the agenda. The member states have officials who preside over certain sectors of their operation—for example, Ministers of Finance, Ministers of Foreign Affairs, etc. These officials are elected or appointed by existing procedures in each country, and it is these individuals who are sent to represent their countries in the European Community's Council. The participants of any given Council meeting depends on the issue being discussed. If the Council intends to discuss the harmonization of corporate taxes, the finance ministers from the twelve EC countries would attend; if agricultural subsidies were discussed, the agricultural ministers would attend, and so on. In reality the Council of Ministers is not a single assembly of people at all, but rather a conglomeration of many groups, each concerned with an individual topic. It has become usual, therefore, to refer to a given assembly of ministers as the "Environment Council," the "Agriculture Council," or the "Consumer Affairs Council," etc., depending on its area of specialty.

Traditionally, the highest representative of a nation is its prime minister or president. These individuals obviously do not normally attend Council meetings. But problems in the 1970s involving the inability of the Council to reach agreements made an assembly of the heads of state appropriate. They have the authority necessary to impose unpopular decisions, and can con-

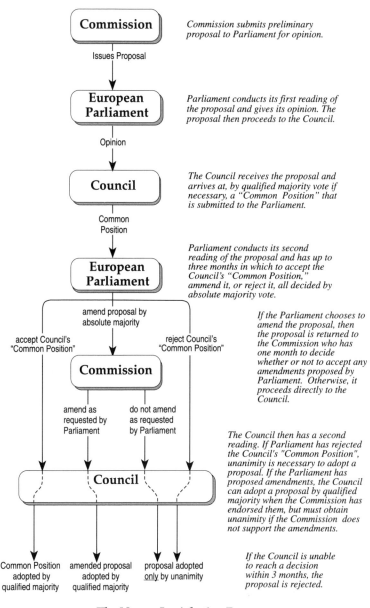

Commission

Commission submits preliminary proposal to Parliament for opinion.

Issues Proposal

European Parliament

Parliament conducts its first reading of the proposal and gives its opinion. The proposal then proceeds to the Council.

Opinion

Council

The Council receives the proposal and arrives at, by qualified majority vote if necessary, a "Common Position" that is submitted to the Parliament.

Common Position

European Parliament

Parliament conducts its second reading of the proposal and has up to three months in which to accept the Council's "Common Position," amend it, or reject it, all decided by absolute majority vote.

amend proposal by absolute majority

accept Council's "Common Position"

reject Council's "Common Position"

If the Parliament chooses to amend the proposal, then the proposal is returned to the Commission who has one month to decide whether or not to accept any amendments proposed by Parliament. Otherwise, it proceeds directly to the Council.

Commission

amend as requested by Parliament

do not amend as requested by Parliament

The Council then has a second reading. If Parliament has rejected the Council's "Common Position", unanimity is necessary to adopt a proposal. If the Parliament has proposed amendments, the Council can adopt a proposal by qualified majority when the Commission has endorsed them, but must obtain unanimity if the Commission does not support the amendments.

Council

Common Position adopted by qualified majority

amended proposal adopted by qualified majority

proposal adopted only by unanimity

If the Council is unable to reach a decision within 3 months, the proposal is rejected.

**The Newer Legislative Process
—the "Cooperation Procedure"**

vince political oppositions in their country of the need to do so. This group of top government representatives is called the European Council. It was invented by the Heads of State themselves when, in 1974, the President of France suggested that the heads of state or government should begin convening on a regularly scheduled basis to discuss important matters regarding the Community. Though the European Council has existed since 1974, it did not gain legal standing in the Community's treaties until 1986 when it was formalized by the Single European Act.

The European Council has met at least twice a year since 1974, normally in Brussels, and has become the ultimate power within the Community. If a proposal is particularly difficult and a Council of junior ministers (i.e., ministers of agriculture, environment, etc.) is unable to reach a consensus on it, it may be passed up to the Council at the foreign minister level. If a consensus is not reached there, it must be considered by the European Council. Meetings of the European Council are sometimes referred to as European "summits."

The Council of Ministers meets only a few times a year, and is not resident in Brussels. To maintain a constant presence, each member state appoints a Permanent Representative who resides in Brussels and continually interacts with the EC institutions. This group of delegates is called the Committee of Permanent Representatives, or COREPER. The members of COREPER work with the Commission to try to get proposals into final shape before submitting them to the Council. This process helps ensure that the minor differences are worked out of a proposal before it reaches the Council, enabling the Council's ministers to concentrate on the more important issues. The Permanent Representatives also assist the European Council by preparing issues for them to consider and by providing other administrative support.

Operation of the Council

—Voting

Throughout the years, voting in the Council has been conducted in various ways, but historically most decisions have been reached unanimously or not at all. As we have seen, before 1966, the Treaty of Rome required a unanimous vote for virtually any decision and thereafter a simple majority basis was allowed. But in 1966 a crisis occurred when France refused to accept a proposal it disliked. This led to an agreement known as the "Luxembourg Compromise," whereby a state was allowed to veto a proposal it felt conflicted with its national interests. The veto was intended to be used only when vital national issues were at stake, but unfortunately it was sometimes used for short-lived political reasons (such as impending elections), and did little to enhance the Community's good standing.

The Single European Act corrected this problem by removing the right of veto and establishing qualified-majority voting as the rule, rather than the exception, whenever a general policy has been agreed to (such as the single-market program). Under the qualified-majority system, a proposal is passed if it receives a *qualified* majority of the votes—this being defined as 54 out of a possible 76 votes. The number of Council votes a country is allocated depends upon its population. Presently, the twelve member nations are assigned voting capacity as shown in the table below.

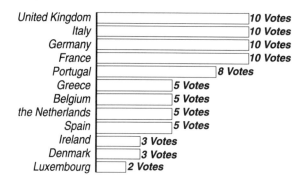

Number of Council Votes per Member State (76 Total)

By studying the number of votes allocated to each member state, it can be seen that the majority-voting system makes it impossible for any single country, or pair of countries, to prevent a proposal from being approved. At the same time, the system requires that at least two large countries vote for a particular proposal in order for it to be approved.

The Council may approve a proposal by qualified majority if it accepts it just as written by the Commission. It can change or reject the proposal if it decides unanimously to do so, but it may not alter a proposal unless it undividedly agrees on the alteration. The most that can be accomplished without a unanimous vote is acceptance of a proposition (provided it receives at least 54 of the 76 votes) exactly as written by the Commission. For propositions concerning issues of taxation, professional qualifications, and the "rights and interest of employees," a unanimous vote is still required. These subjects are considered to be of such a sensitive nature that all member states should support the proposition, or it should not be implemented.

—*The Council Presidency*

The Presidency of the Council is given, successively, to each member nation for a term of six months. During those six months, the ascribed country's minister of foreign affairs serves as the president of the Council, acting as the spokesperson for the EC and setting the period's agenda. The order that the countries assume the presidency is determined alphabetically by the name of each country in its mother language, i.e., België (Dutch) or Belgique (French), Danmark, Deutschland, Ellas (Hellas), España, France, Ireland, Italia, Luxembourg, Nederland, Portugal, United Kingdom.

At Council meetings in Brussels, each representative moves around the rectangular table one seat in a clockwise direction after each change of Presidency. A representative from the Commission also attends Council meetings and sits opposite the president, who always sits at the head of the table. The seating arrangement and rotation scenario are portrayed in the figure on the facing page.

This alphabetical system of determining the Council presidency was used during the round of twelve presidencies from 1987 to 1992. Since the spring of 1992, a small complication has been added to the system.

Since most work concerning agriculture is generally conducted during the first half of the year, and items concerning the budget are primarily attended to during the second, the responsibilities of the president are different during the first and second halves of the year. To prevent a given nation from always assuming the presidency during one half of the year and never the other, each year's pair of presidents will now switch terms until 1998. Thus rather than Belgium holding the presidency for the first half of 1993 and Denmark holding it in the second (strict alphabetical order), Denmark will have the presidency during the first half of 1993, Belgium during the second; Greece in the first half of 1994, Germany in the second, and so on. This enables each EC country to be president during both seasonal agendas.

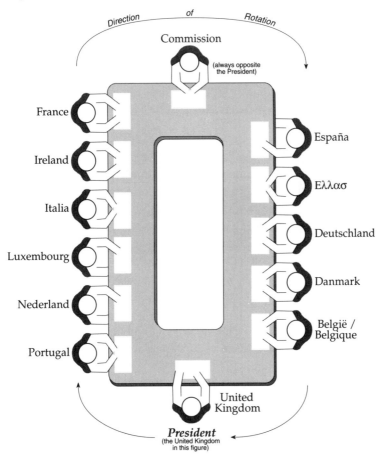

**The Rotation of the Council Presidency
and the Council Seating Arrangement**

The Commission of the European Community

The Commission serves as the Community's executive—the institution that is responsible for administering the laws and affairs of the EC. As mentioned already, it is the birthplace of all proposed EC legislation and, therefore, of all EC law. Nothing may be considered or approved by the Council unless it has been formally submitted by the Commission. The subject matter of the proposals, as well as the time and order in which they are submitted, is entirely decided by the Commission. The members of the Commission are to act on the behalf of the European Community as a whole, and they are expected to uphold the Community's plea when protectionist or other nationalistic issues arise.

The Commission's duties can be divided into three broad categories as follows:

  i) to initiate EC policy,

 ii) to act as guardian and enforcer of the EC treaties,

iii) to put accepted EC policies into operation (under authority granted by the Council).

Presently, the Commission is composed of 17 Members. The number of commissioners from each member state is loosely based on population with France, Germany, Italy, Spain and the United Kingdom each appointing two, and the remaining member nations appointing one apiece. Members of the Commission are chosen by the mutual agreement of the national governments, and serve four year terms (they are not elected). The European Parliament is tasked with ensuring that the Commission remains true to its obligations. The Parliament is the only body that has supervisory powers over the Commission, and it may force the Commission to resign if it determines this is necessary (a capability the Parliament has never needed to perform).

The Commission is headed by a president who is appointed from within its ranks. The president officially serves for two years, but this term is often extended to four years so it parallels the four-year terms of the other commissioners. Six vice-presidents are similarly appointed, and also serve two year terms. The Commission is based in Brussels and is presently inhabiting several offices within the city while awaiting the completion of a new building sometime in 1993. An administrative staff of approximately 17,000, which is divided into some 22 area intensive groups called Directorates-General (DG), supports the Commission. The various Directorates-General are each assigned a number, and are referred to as DG I, DG IV, DG XV, etc. The Directorate General may be thought of as the Community's civil service. The leaders of each DG section are specialists in their field, providing the expertise that is necessary for the Community to make wise decisions. The staff is based largely in Brussels, and to a lesser extent in Luxembourg. Approximately 2,500 of these people are linguists who manage the Community's enormous translation needs. The table below shows the responsibilities of the various DGs.

Directorate Number (DG)	Directorate Responsibility
I	External Relations
II	Economic and financial affairs
III	Internal market and industrial affairs
IV	Competition
V	Employment, social affairs and education
VI	Agriculture
VII	Transport
VIII	Development
IX	Personnel and administration
X	Information, communication and culture
XI	Environment, consumer protection, nuclear safety
XII	Science, research and development
XIII	Telecommunications, computers and innovation
XIV	Fisheries
XV	Financial institutions and company law
XVI	Regional Policy
XVII	Energy
XVIII	Credit and investments
XIX	Budgets
XX	Financial control
XXI	Customs union and indirect taxation
XXII	Coordination of structural instruments

Each commissioner is assigned specific responsibilities by the Commission president based on his or her qualifications. The minister appointed to oversee transportation becomes, in essence, the EC minister of transportation, and will interact directly with the Directorate-General of transportation. If the Commission desires to write a new proposal on trucking regulations, the minister of transportation will oversee the necessary draft proposal. The minister will work closely with the Directorate General for Transport, and information will be solicited from the widest possible base including: member governments, trucking firms, environmentalists, and anybody else who has relevant opinions on the subject. When the proposal is finished, all 17 commissioners must agree that its contents are reasonable before submitting it to the Council.

The Commission is responsible for ensuring that the terms of the Community's treaties, as well as its laws, are not violated. The European Coal and Steel Community's early provisions for disciplining those who digressed from its laws were complex, cumbersome and slow. Wishing to avoid these negative characteristics, the disciplinary provisions written into the Treaty of Rome were simpler and sterner, and have proven themselves to be more effective. The Commission is the wielder of these enforcement provisions, and as guardian of the EC treaties, is obligated to use them whenever an infringement of Community policy occurs. The Commission investigates any presumed offense, either on its own initiative or when brought to its attention from an outside source. Most infringements involve one of two scenarios: either a member state has incorrectly incorporated a Community directive into its national laws (often due only to misinterpretation), or a member state has failed completely to incorporate a directive into its law. Infractions by companies or individuals span a broader range, and may consist of anything from discriminatory hiring practices to illegally controlling competition.

When the Commission finds that an offense has indeed occurred, it will ask the member state, where the infraction took place, to comment on the occurrence—generally within two months. If the offense is serious (i.e., it affects the proper functioning of the common market), the period for comment is much shorter. If the Commission cannot be convinced by the member state's comments that the disputed practice does not violate Community policy, it will issue a *reasoned opinion* that the member state is obligated to obey. It also has the power to impose fines on individuals or companies. If the accused member state does not comply or force the offender to comply within the time limit specified in the opinion, the Commission may ask the Court of Justice to conduct proceedings on the matter. Once a judgment is reached by the Court of Justice, it is binding on all involved parties.

The final primary duty of the Commission is to ensure that EC policies that have been adopted by the Council are properly put into operation. To do this, the Commission has been given limited legislative powers. The Council must issue new legislation concerning matters of broad policy, but the Commission has law making authority in situations that are either defined by existing Council legislation, or are explicitly defined by the Community's treaties. Once specific policies are in place, the Commission is responsible for enacting rules that define the specific details. Consequently, legislation issued by the Commission is usually administrative or technical in nature. The majority of the Community's laws are these Commission-issued regulations.

The EC has four special-purpose funds that are managed by the Commission. These funds provide money for specific needs, and account for a large majority of the Community's budgeted expenses. The funds and their goals are as follows:

- The European Regional Development Fund (ERDF) was set up in 1975 to alleviate imbalances within the community. Its purpose is to provide money to help the less developed member states of the EC improve their infrastructure. The establishment of the fund, and the large amounts of money that have passed through it into the eager coffers of the poorer EC nations such as Greece, Portugal and Spain, demonstrate the EC's determination to alleviate regional imbalances within its borders.

- The European Social Fund (ESF) was established by the Treaty of Rome, and furnishes money for grants that provide vocational training for EC workers.

- The European Agricultural Guidance and Guarantee Fund (EAGGF) endows funding for all provisions concerning agriculture subsidies and price supports. It provides the money for the Common Agricultural Policy (CAP), which is the EC's single largest expenditure.

- And finally, the European Development Fund (EDF) serves as the EC's source of foreign aid, giving grants to needy third-world countries.

The Interaction of the Council and Commission

International organizations have always been at risk of not having any real power if an issue becomes unappetizing to one or more of its member nations. To circumvent this problem, the Treaty of Rome carefully defines many mechanisms that are intended to evenly match the powers within the Community. The forces between the Council and the Commission were carefully designed to balance the desires of the individual member nations against those of the Community. These checks and balances occur in many ways.

To begin with, it should be reemphasized that the Council can only deliberate on proposals that have been submitted to it by the Commission. Given the Commission's cause, its proposals will, by definition, be aimed at serving the common interest of the EC. The Council may not enact any legislation without first obtaining a proposal from the Commission. This means that the Commission has the permanent right and duty to initiate action within the system. If it fails to do so, the Council becomes paralyzed, and progress comes to a standstill.

Another way the Council is encouraged to reach "Community decisions" is through the provisions in the EC's legislation procedures that allow the Council to amend a proposal only if it decides unanimously to do so. If the Council can agree undividedly on an amendment or alteration, it may make the desired change. But if the Council ministers have any disagreement among themselves, the most they can do is accept the Commission's proposal without amendment.

Since all proposals must be initiated by the Commission, and the Council may not alter them unless every member state agrees, a guarantee is provided that member states cannot impose a measure upon another without the support of the Commission. For example, if a majority in the Council would like to pass a law that would seriously damage the economy of Luxembourg, tiny Luxembourg can firmly and successfully oppose its much larger neighbors as long as the Commission remains on its side. The Commission, by definition, should never support any proposal that would seriously damage an EC country. This ensures that Luxembourg's interests will be upheld—an important guarantee, especially to the smaller member states, who might otherwise be at the mercy of their larger partners.

Lastly, since the members of the Council are generally not unreasonable, aristocratic thugs, they would prefer to agree than disagree whenever possible. Being the odd man out can be both difficult and embarrassing. Since a proposal can be adopted by majority vote, the chance of a divergent minister being outvoted is a very real prospect. This possibility often tends to persuade ministers to abandon extreme positions, making decisions easier to obtain while helping to preserve the Community's integrity.

Through these various mechanisms, the Commission is able to play a central role within the Council, acting as a type of "EC catalyst." It applies the persuasion and influence necessary to fabricate policies that are acceptable to all the member states, while being sure to take into account their individual essential interests.

The European Parliament—The Democratic Voice

The European Parliament was initially an appointed body, but since 1979 it has been elected by European citizens. It can be illustratively compared to the US Congress, though it is organized by political party rather than by nationality (or by state, in the case of the US Congress). Its origins go back to the Treaty of Rome, which modified the already established *Parliamentary Assembly* by transforming it from an ECSC institution into a common institution of the ECSC, the EEC and Euratom. Though the Treaty of Rome continued to call it the "Assembly," the title "European Parliament" has been used since 1962 and was officially changed in 1986. The Assembly was established as a purely consultative body, but through the years Parliament has gained additional powers, primarily through the Single European Act's "cooperation procedure." Despite these recent enhancements, the strength of the European Parliament remains in its influence—it has few genuine legislative powers.

Today, the European Parliament consists of 518 members who are headed by one president and fourteen vice-presidents. Members of Parliament are arranged in Community-level political groupings. Each member state is allowed to send a certain number of representatives to the Parliament, the amount being roughly determined by its population. As shown by the chart to the left, the largest member nations are allowed 81 MEPs (Member of European Parliament), while tiny Luxembourg is allotted only six. The European Council recently allowed Germany some additional members to account for the reunification with former East Germany.

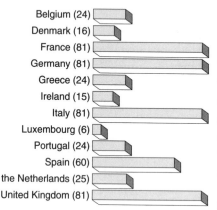

Belgium (24)
Denmark (16)
France (81)
Germany (81)
Greece (24)
Ireland (15)
Italy (81)
Luxembourg (6)
Portugal (24)
Spain (60)
the Netherlands (25)
United Kingdom (81)

Number of Parliament Members per Nation

It is important to keep in mind that the members of the Parliament sit according to political party—not nationality. There is officially no such thing as the Spanish Members of the European Parliament, or the Danish Members of the European Parliament. Even though the various members are elected by voters from a certain nation, once elected they are not accountable to that nation—they should act on their own behalf in a manner that they feel will benefit the Community as a whole. This lack of national segregation ensures that the Parliament is truly a fully-integrated, Community-level institution.

A multitude of political groups exists within the European Parliament that covers the political spectrum from left to right. The figure on the next page depicts the Parliament's composition.

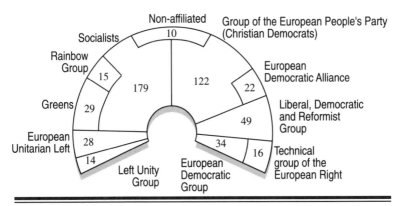

The Parties of the European Parliament

	Total	B Belgium	DK Denmark	D Germany	GR Greece	E Spain	F France	IRL Ireland	I Italy	L Luxembourg	NL Netherlands	P Portugal	UK United Kingdom
Socialist Group	179	8	4	31	9	27	22	1	14	2	8	7	46
Group of the European People's Party (Christian Democratic Group)	122	7	2	32	10	17	6	4	27	3	10	3	1
Liberal, Democratic and Reformist Group	49	4	3	4	-	6	13	2	3	1	4	9	-
European Democratic Group	34	-	2	-	-	-	-	-	-	-	-	-	32
The Green Group in the European Parliament	29	3	-	7	-	1	8	-	7	-	2	1	
Group of the United European Left	28	-	1	-	1	4	1	-	22	-	-	-	-
Group of the European Democratic Alliance	22	-	-	-	1	2	13	6	-	-	-	-	-
Technical Group of the European Right	16	1	-	5	-	-	10	-	-	-	-	-	-
Rainbow Group in the European Parliament	15	1	4	1	-	2	1	1	3	-	-	1	1
Left Unity Group	14	-	-	-	3	-	7	1	-	-	-	3	-
Non-affiliated	10	-	-	1	-	1	1	-	5	-	1	-	1
Total	518	24	16	81	24	60	81	15	81	6	25	24	81

* Data represents situation on February 18, 1991. Source Eurostat.

The top portion shows the number of MEPs that sit in each political party and indicates the parties' relative left to right political orientation (left—more radical or liberal causes, right—more conservative or traditional causes). The table on the lower half of the page shows the total number of representatives each member state may elect, as well as the chosen parties of these representatives. The various political groups in the European Parliament have arisen, among other reasons, to gain access to EC political funds, and their composition reflects the political groupings found in the member countries.

The operation of the Parliament

The job of the European Parliament, and of each of its members, is to think and work on behalf of the citizens of the Community as a whole. It should attempt to improve the workings of the EC government, and expose injustices and bureaucratic inefficiencies. One of the Parliament's most fundamental duties is to provide an educated opinion on all proposals under consideration by the EC legislative machine. Each proposal from the Commission is presented to the Parliament en route to the Council. The members of Parliament are divided into 18 specialized committees that cover topics from research and technology to fisheries. Depending upon the subject of a proposal, it is given to the appropriate parliamentary committee who then thoroughly researches it and publishes a report on the topic. Based upon the report, the Parliament votes on the proposal, and subsequently submits its opinion to the Council and Commission.

Full European Parliament meetings are normally held in Strasbourg, France, for one week each month. Occasional special meetings, usually of shorter duration, may also be held to discuss particular topics such as the budget. Between each week-long Parliamentary session, two weeks are reserved for committee meetings. The remaining week of the month is used for meetings by party members with their political groups. The committee and political-group meetings are held in Brussels, while Parliament's Secretariat, with some 3,500 staff members, is in Luxembourg.

For years, national pride prevented the official designation of any one city as the home of the European Parliament—the EC countries could not agree who would receive this honor. Recently, much to the joy of the French government, Strasbourg (France) was named the official seat of the European Parliament. This situation has forced the rather awkward logistics of having full European Parliament sessions in Strasbourg and committee meetings in Brussels, while the Parliament's secretariat remains in Luxembourg.

The primary responsibilities of Parliament can be broken up into four distinct pieces: a legislative component, a budgetary component, a supervisory component, and a role as a political driving force within the EC. Each of these elements are described in the following sections.

The Parliament as a legislative body

Although the Parliament does not have any explicit legislative powers, it can, and certainly does, influence the legislative process. This is accomplished by stating its opinion on draft proposals from the Commission and by requesting that the Commission alter its proposals to closer fit Parliamentary opinion.

The "cooperation procedure" requires that any proposal that the Parliament wishes to amend or reject may not become law unless the Parliamentary amendments are incorporated, or the Council obtains a unanimous vote to deviate from the Parliament's requests. Although the "cooperation procedure" does not apply in every case, it was used exclusively during the effort to establish the single market, and has enabled the Parliament to have more influence in the final make-up of Community legislation.

The Single European Act additionally augmented the Parliament's power by a provision it calls the "power of assent". This provision requires that any proposed EC agreement, concerning international association or cooperation, must be reviewed and accepted by the Parliament before concluded.

Even if recent gains have increased its influence in the legislative process, it should be pointed out that the European Parliament is still unsatisfied with its role. It continues to cite the presence of a "democratic deficit," in the EC's system, and uses it as rational for requesting additional powers. Parliament's stated point of view, ever since it was directly elected in 1979, is that the power to enact legislation should be shared between Parliament and the Council.[5] Members of Parliament see such a sharing of responsibility as the best way of ensuring that the voice of Parliament, and therefore of EC citizens, is heard and used to influence the direction of the Community. Many Members of Parliament have made it known that they intend to exert political pressure to increase the legislative powers of Parliament, and at the same time will use all possibilities open to them to make the Parliament's influence felt in the legislative process.

The Parliament as a Budgetary Power

Parliament is the institution that adopts the Community's budget. It can also reject a proposed budget—which has happened twice in the past (in 1979 and 1985)—requiring the budgetary procedure to begin again. The Community's budget is initially prepared by the Commission, and is then sent back and forth between the Parliament and the Council. The Parliament and the Council together direct the Community's expenses. In matters regarding "compulsory" expenditures, the Council has the final word. "Compulsory" expenditures are defined as those that come as a direct consequence of EC legislation, such as agricultural subsidies. The Parliament may recommend that modifications be made to compulsory expenditures if it is dissatisfied with them, and these recommendations are often accepted by the Council. In all non-compulsory expenditures, the Parliament has the final word. Since non-compulsory expenditures account for approximately 20 to 30 percent of the total EC budget (ECU 55 million in 1991), this role involves more than a trivial amount of money.

The Parliament may, within confines prescribed by the EC's treaties, modify how the money it is in charge of is apportioned. In general, it has control over the portion of the Community's budget concerning administrative costs and certain operational expenditures. Its power over these expenses is significant because its appropriations influence the Community's developmental path. By increasing or decreasing expenditures in certain areas,

---

5.   Noël, Emile. 1988. *Working Together: The Institutions of the European Community,* Luxembourg: Office of the Official Publications of the European Communities.

such as in social or regional aid, or by allowing or disallowing new efforts in research, construction, or energy development, the Parliament can help decide in which areas the Community will rapidly develop and in which areas progress will come more slowly.

The Parliament may reallocate expenditures between the various beneficiaries and can, within certain limits, increase the amount spent in a given area. It may not, however, increase the total amount of Community expenditure. Increases in spending limits can only be obtained by cutting expenses somewhere else.

The Parliament as Supervisor of the Commission

The Parliament endeavors to ensure that the interests of the European people play the foremost role in the Commission's program, and that lobbying interests of individual governments do not excessively influence Commission decisions. One way this oversight occurs is through the Parliament's opinions on Commission proposals. Additionally, Members of Parliament maintain an awareness of the activities of the Commission and Council, and may voice their concerns through verbal and written questions to those institutions. Regularly scheduled "Question Times," where Members of the Parliament can ask questions of other Community officials, have proven very popular, and are an effective method for MEPs to influence the other EC institutions.

The ultimate display of disapproval held by the Parliament is one that it has so far never deemed necessary to use. It may dismiss, i.e., replace, the entire Commission by adopting a "motion of censure." This requires a vote whereby at least two-thirds of the Members of Parliament choose to replace the Commission. This action is limited to replacing the entire Commission as a group. The Parliament does not have the ability to replace only one or a few commissioners individually.

The Parliament as a Political Driving Force

Finally, and perhaps most importantly, is the role of Parliament as the political force representing the 342 million citizens of the Community. Though this appointment is less concrete than the legislative or budgetary functions, it is as vital. Since its members are directly elected by the European people, Parliament is the leading forum of European opinion. It reflects the political and national sentiments of the twelve EC countries, and provides an atmosphere teeming with ambition. It is often the source of initiative for new proposals or revisions to existing policies. Parliament was the decisive factor that persuaded the Community governments to endorse the Single European Act, and requests from Parliament also led to important conferences on monetary and political union.

The European Court of Justice

The Court of Justice is the EC's parallel to the United State's Supreme Court. Created by the Treaty of Rome to replace the ECSC's Court of Justice with a Community wide judicial institution, it is the final mediator when a question of law exists in the EC. Its judgment is binding on all parties involved. Physically, the Court is located in Luxembourg, and consists of 13 judges—one from each member state plus one additional judge to eliminate the possibility of an even vote. The judges are appointed by mutual agreement of the governments of the member states, and serve six year terms. The terms are staggered among the judges to ensure that the Court is partially replaced every three years. Along with the six judges, there are six Advocates-General who assist the judges. The Advocates-General also serve six year terms.

The fundamental tasks of the Court are to ensure a uniform interpretation of Community law and its application, to evaluate the legality of legislation adopted by the Council and the Commission, and to provide rulings on Community law when requested to do so by any of the member state's national courts. In fulfilling the second obligation, the Court may declare void any legal instrument that has been adopted by the Commission or the Council if it finds it incompatible with standing Community law. A request to begin proceedings regarding the compatibility of a law may come from a Community institution, a member state or any directly concerned individual. If the Court determines that the case is well founded and that indeed changes are necessary, an order, or judgment, is given to the offending nation. Officials in the cited member state are expected to make the necessary changes to comply with the Court's order. If a domestic law must be changed, national officials are required to alter it so that it complies with the Community's laws. Courts in the member states are obligated to ensure that compliance with the Court of Justice's judgments are practiced. If a member state feels that another member state has failed to comply with an obligation under the Treaties, it may request that the Court of Justice make a binding ruling that requires the faulted member state to change its practices.

One of the most notable cases involving a member state being forced to change its law involved the famous German beer purity laws *(reinheitsgebot)* and exported beer from other EC countries. The centuries-old laws allow only products containing hops, malted barley, yeast and water to be designated *beer.* Since the imported beers contained additional ingredients, the German law disqualified them from being sold in Germany. When the purity law was challenged, the Court of Justice ruled that it was not based on "essential requirements" because the Germans allowed the ingredients they disapproved of, in the imported beers, to be present in other drink products sold in Germany.[6] There was nothing essentially wrong with the disputed ingredients—they just opposed German tradition. Thus, the imported beers were allowed to be sold in Germany.

To help the Court of Justice manage its heavy caseload, an additional court was initiated in the Community in September 1989. Called the "Court of First Instance," it was founded to hear and provide judgments for certain classes of action, particularly those regarding competition laws, at their first instance. The Court of First Instance, enables the Court of Justice to better concentrate on its primary obligation of ensuring consistent interpretation and application of Community law.

As the most independent institution in the EC—an essential characteristic of an impartial court of law—the Court of Justice can force Community and member state policies to coincide with the aspirations of the original treaties. It is not prone to waiver from member state pressure or other variables, and is thus, one of the most important advocates of free-trade in the Community.

---

6. Judgment of the European Court of Justice, case 178/84, Commission of the European Communities v. Federal Republic of Germany.

The European Investment Bank

An additional EC institution, that has not been mentioned yet, is the European Investment Bank (EIB). The Bank was established by the Treaty of Rome, and serves as the EC's financial institution. It is a non-profit establishment that raises funds by issuing bonds and other financial instruments in the world's financial markets, and then loans these funds to investors who have projects that will contribute to the growth of the Community. The bank favors projects involving the development of the less-favored regions of the Community and the construction of transport and communications infrastructures. Loans are made at an interest rate that reflects the cost of the funds—no profit is added on.

Financing the Community

The funds necessary for financing EC activities have come entirely from resources within the EC since 1975. This self-sufficiency is achieved through a system of "own resources," which has enabled the Community to receive income based upon its own authority, freeing it from dependency on outside sources of income. Before the gradual introduction of this system, the Community was financed through contributions from the member states.

The resources from which the Community receives income consist primarily of duties collected under the Common Customs Tariff, agricultural levies charged on agricultural imports from non-EC countries, levies derived from sugar, and funds that come from the 1.4% of Value-added taxes (VAT) that have been allocated to the EC since 1986. Revenue from VAT has evolved into the primary source of funds for the EC, accounting for 60% of the Community budget in 1990.

An additional source of revenue was introduced with the Single European Act, which is based on the gross national products of each of the individual member states. Under this plan, the amount paid to the EC, by each member state, corresponds to its ability to pay. It is somewhat like income tax—those with more income (i.e., higher GNPs), pay more. The Community's total budget in 1991 was about ECU 58.5 million, which represents only 1.2 percent of the combined gross domestic product of the member states.

5

1992 and the
Single European Market

If men would consider not so much where they differ, as wherein they agree, there would be far less of uncharitableness and angry feeling in the world.

— Joseph Addison

A t midnight December 31, 1992, boy scouts, in cities and towns all across Europe, lit bonfires to signify the official launch of the EC's single European market. This milestone marked the end of the project's frantic implementation period, but is only the beginning of changes that will continue to reshape Europe for years.

Whether it is called the "single market," the "common market," or the "internal market," these names all denote the same thing—a twelve-nation marketplace in which duties, tariffs and quotas have been removed, and obstacles toward the free movement of people, money and goods have been abolished. Rules and conditions that govern the way business is done have been radically changed, and wherever necessary national idiosyncrasies have been replaced by Community-wide standards. Implementation of the single market involved eight years of frenzied preparations and legislative proceedings. This chapter reveals the approach that was used to put it in place, and examines the motivations that led to its development.

Before the Single Market

Protectionism

Before the reasoning behind the 1992 single-market project can be explained, the concept of *protectionism* must be understood. Protectionism occurs when a government supports its domestic industries by restricting and/or taxing imports to discourage foreign competition. Another, somewhat disguised, form of protectionism occurs when nations manipulate their national standards to make the sale of foreign goods difficult or impossible. Before the single market, such practices were very popular in Europe. Germany, for example, denied the sale of a particular French liqueur simply because it did not have enough alcohol to satisfy German specifications. It was a safe, perfectly acceptable product, yet was denied access to the German market. This refusal, though somewhat veiled, is blatant protectionism. Often, laws claiming to be necessary for consumer safety were nothing less than attempts to protect domestic industries—purity laws, bottling restrictions, labeling and packaging laws, ingredient bans, alcohol content limits—all have been used to limit external competition. But, as many European countries have discovered, protectionism does not always yield beneficial results.

A simple example of how protectionism is meant to work, followed by an example of why it can become self-defeating, is instructive. In its purest form, a country might practice protectionism in the automobile market by adding a surtax of, say, 30% to all foreign automobiles sold in the country. Domestic manufacturers would not be subject to the surtax, and would thus hold a distinct advantage over their foreign competitors. The cost of the surtax would be borne by either an increase in imported car prices or a decrease in profit margins for foreign manufacturers—both of which hurt foreign firms' ability to remain competitive.

In the past, many national governments have successfully used tactics like this to boost their domestic industries—but the effectiveness of protectionism has dwindled as the importance of technology in business has grown. Imagine a country that decides to try to help its ailing computer industry by adding a 30% tax to the price of imported computer equipment. This sounds plausible initially—it is the same action that was taken regarding the automobiles in the previous example. But in this case the consequences of such an action would likely cause more damage than good. The difference is that many companies need advanced computers to stay in business. By forcing them to buy inferior domestic computers or pay abnormally high prices for sophisticated foreign equipment—the same equipment that competitors in other nations can buy cheaper—the protectionist government has seriously handicapped its industries that depend upon advanced computer technology (such as banking or aerospace). The 1980s were littered with incidents of European businesses becoming uncompetitive or incurring high costs due to protectionist laws. As a result, EC firms found it increasingly difficult to remain competitive in the world marketplace, and sagging economic indicators verified the negative effect of their difficulties.

Fragmentation

A single word expresses many of the European Community's economic troubles before the single market—fragmentation. On a global scale, the populations of the individual member states are relatively small, ranging from just 360,000 in Luxembourg to about 79 million in reunified Germany. Even as the EC's largest member, Germany's market is still less than half the size of the Japanese, and has only a quarter as many consumers as the United States. But taken together, the EC represents a free market of 340 million people—the largest in the world (the US, by comparison, has a population of about 250 million). Logically, one might think that the largest free market in the world should have a proportionate share of the world's strongest companies. This, however, is not so. European companies have had difficulty keeping up with their competitors abroad, and few possess the capacity of the best American and Japanese corporations. A primary reason for their difficulties is market fragmentation.

Market fragmentation occurs when business conditions vary across a given territory due to changes in requirements. Differing requirements cause complications and expenses for companies who must comply with them. Any market, the US included, has a certain amount of market fragmentation, but Europe has always had considerably more than either the US or Japan. To be fair, it must be pointed out that, unlike its main competitors, Europe has extensive cultural differences that tend to perpetuate fragmentation. Still, unnecessary regulations, not cultural differences, have caused many of the free-trade barriers that have burdened European industry for decades.

Until recently, European companies wishing to sell outside their domestic market had to cope with an incredible variety of technical requirements. National regulations forced companies to design products in accordance with many standards, making it difficult, if not impossible, to sell a uniformly designed product throughout the EC. Because of these demands, industry largely reflected the divisions delineated by a map of Europe. Specialized divisions that dealt individually with each national market became the European norm. Though many companies were operating in several Community countries, they were unable to optimize their production activities because each national division was run differently than the others. As a result, European products ended up costing more, and few large companies—companies capable of competing with the enormous corporations in the US and Japan—developed on European soil.

Fragmentation also handicapped the efficiency of research and development. As a whole, the member states of the European Community have tended to spend as much on research and development as Japan. But because these expenditures were uncoordinated, the research money was not used efficiently. Research spending on a national basis resulted in work being unnecessarily duplicated, as scientists and engineers in one EC country repeated research other member states had already paid for. Moreover, large research efforts, like those possible in the US and Japan, were generally not possible in Europe because they were too expensive for the resources of any individual EC nation. By pooling the research funds of all EC countries this problem would be eliminated, making formerly impractical efforts possible.

In short, fragmentation caused Europe to use its collective resources inefficiently, which led to extensive costs being imposed in all areas of economic activity. In the end, these costs were borne by European companies who were unable to remain globally competitive and by European consumers who were forced to accept less choice and increased prices.

The Motive of the 1992 Single-Market Program

Estimated Costs of the Fragmented Market

In 1988, a study was carried out at the request of the Commission to attempt to ascertain the cost of not having a unified market in Europe. This study was conducted by many independent economic experts and was led by Mr. Paolo Cecchini. The results of this study, which is referred to as the Cecchini Report, can be summarized by the following chart:

Projected Savings from the Common Market

Total savings from the abolition of administrative formalities and border controls	ECU 13 to 24 billion
Potential savings from opening up public procurement markets	±ECU 17.5 billion
Effect on the Labor Market	2 to 5 million new jobs
Savings from increasing the scale of production of manufactured goods	2% of GDP

From these findings, the study arrived at the following conclusions:

(i)   The total potential economic gain to the Community as a whole, from the completion of the internal market, is estimated to be ECU 200 billion or more, expressed in 1988 prices. This would add about 5% to the Community's gross domestic product.

(ii)   The study further shows that the predicted effects of EC market integration will in the medium-term:

  (a)   deflate consumer prices by an average of 6% while boosting output, employment and living standards,

  (b)   produce economies in public sector costs equivalent to 2.2% of GDP and boost the EC's trade with other countries by around 1% of GDP.

(iii)   The direct costs of frontier formalities, including associated administrative costs for both the private and public sectors, are estimated to be 1.8% of the value of goods traded within the Community. To this must be added the costs to industry of other identifiable barriers to a complete internal market, such as differing national technical regulations governing the manufacture and marketing of products, which are estimated to average a little under 2% of companies' total costs. The combined total of all these savings then represents about 3.5% of industrial value-added.

(iv)   There are substantial, unexploited, potential economies of scale in European industry. It is estimated that about one-third of European industry could profit from cost reductions ranging from 1% to 7%, depending on the sector concerned. Aggregate cost savings from improved economies of scale would thus amount to something on the order of 2% of GDP.[7]

These figures succeeded in alerting politicians to the inefficiencies of "non-Europe," but the benefits of a single market were by no means a new revelation. The idea of a coordinated European economy based on a common market has been a core part of the vision of the EC since the Treaty of Rome was signed in 1957. A passage from the opening lines of the treaty clearly shows that the Community's founders intended a common market to be at the heart of the unification process.

> *"The Community shall have as its task, by establishing a common market and progressively approximating the economic policies of member states, to promote throughout the Community a harmonious development of economic activities, a continuous and balanced expansion, an increase in stability, an accelerated raising of the standard of living and closer relations between the States belonging to it."*

Yet, in spite of this early call to establish a common market, true progress remained elusive. Even as late as 1985, nearly thirty years after the treaty was written, few steps had been taken to permanently dismantle national trade barriers. The 1968 Customs Union did successfully remove internal customs duties, but its advances were essentially annulled during the 1973 to 1984 period of "Eurosclerosis." When economic hardship came in the 1970s, many European governments reverted to protectionist poli-

---

7.   European Documentation Series, *Europe without Frontiers: Completing the internal market,* 1989, ISBN 92-825-9895-0

cies that favored domestic industries, punished imports, and generally ignored the Community's free-market principles. Why, then, has the 1992 program been successful when attempts over the past 30 years have failed?

"Eurosclerosis" frustrated those who wished to see the Community move forward more ardently. Cries for positive action came from various Community supporters, but these pleas alone were insufficient to overcome political opposition. Only when it became apparent that European countries were steadily falling behind their major non-European rivals economically, did politicians begin to agree that change had become necessary. Seizing this opportunity, Jacques Delors, president of the EC Commission, presented a proposal to the European Parliament on March 12, 1985. This proposal called for the formulation of a precise plan to construct a single European market. It was intended to coerce the EC away from the virtual standstill that had existed for so many years and was presented as an act of urgency. Mr. Delors, among many others, viewed the successful implementation of a single market as crucial. Without it, he said Europe would plunge further behind its global competitors and would be forced to take a second-tier position in the world economy. Such a fate would worsen Europe's already shaky economies and perpetuate its long-standing unemployment and inflation problems.

✳✳✳

It would be pleasant to believe that an effort as grand as Europe's single-market program could be established simply by humanitarianism and desire for greater international harmony. This, however, is not largely the reality. The single market was initiated and exists today because of basic political and economic motivations. Protectionism and fragmentation were gradually eroding the EC's ability to stay competitive in world markets. Officials in Europe recognized that eventually this lack of competitiveness would lead to declining political influence—a prediction which they did not like. Powerful business organizations across the EC began lobbying for governments to take bold actions to streamline the European business environment. Increasingly, it was realized that many of the individual national problems had common causes and that a Community wide solution was necessary to effectively combat them. To prevent Europe from sliding into economic and political ruin, it was agreed that something dramatic had to be done. Gradually, businessmen, economists, national politicians and Members of the European Parliament all began to agree that Europe's ability to compete in modern global markets—and thereby, the future prosperity of Europe—was dependent upon its ability to create a healthy, integrated marketplace. The 1992 program was the result.

The single market can be viewed more as an essential step toward economic survival than as a grand vision of an undivided Europe. After years of delay, the single market was finally put in place due to simple economics. The expense of maintaining the protectionist regulatory structure in Europe became more costly, both economically and politically, than the benefits derived from it. The foremost question in the minds of the authors of the 1992 program was not how to remove international borders for the sake of fellowship, or how to safeguard the welfare of Europe's consumers. Rather, it was how to make European firms emerge that could compete with the IBMs and Mitsubishis of the world so that Europe could regain its economic and political health.

Though the 1992 program was put forth through economic means, the entire exercise had political motivations. Throughout history, governments that wished to increase their influence often used pressure or force. That European governments today have instead chosen cooperation is attributable to fortunate changes. Economic power has surpassed military power as the prime measure of a country's strength, and economic necessities in Europe have led to intergovernmental cooperation of historically unknown proportions.

How the Single Market was Established

The White Paper & the Single European Act

In response to the call to formulate a single-market program, a paper was published by the Commission on June 14, 1985. Written under the authority of Lord Cockfield, a member of the EC Commission and former British businessman, this paper detailed a strategy to systematically convert the Community's twelve national markets into one common market. It was entitled "Completing the Internal Market: White Paper from the Commission to the European Council," and is usually referred to simply as the "White Paper" (*White Paper* is a British term that refers to any official government report because they were originally bound in the same white paper as the pages). Nearly 300 legislative proposals were recommended, which were to be implemented over a period ending December 31, 1992. The end of 1992 was chosen as the deadline because it corresponded to a total program length equal to two four-year Commission terms, or eight years. There was valid concern that focus would be lost if the program were stretched out over three or more Commissions. The White Paper established, for the first time, concrete actions and a timetable toward achieving a truly common internal market in the Community. In late June of 1985, the White Paper was approved by the heads of state in the European Council at a meeting in Milan, Italy.

As brought up previously, the existing EC legislative system had to be modified to ease the implementation of the hundreds of proposals called for by the White Paper. The old requirement, which stated that the Council must reach unanimous agreement before approving a proposal, was often cumbersome and time consuming. Typically, the process was slowed to the pace of the most reluctant member, making advancement unacceptably tedious. If the 1992 deadline were to be met, some form of compromise had to be introduced.

With this in mind, the European Council agreed to amend the EC's treaties as required and in 1986, the necessary legislation was adopted. Officially entitled "The Single Act: A new frontier for Europe," the "Single European Act," was born. At first, problems with ratification were encountered due to conflicts with national constitutions, particularly in Ireland and Denmark. But these conflicts were eventually overcome and on July 1, 1987, after ratification by each of the twelve member state's parliaments, the Single European Act entered into force. It set out the general reforms necessary to establish a single market and required the member nations to bring their laws into accordance with those of the EC.

The Single European Act was the first major revision to the

Treaty of Rome. It officially adopted the plan laid out by the White Paper and formally committed the Community toward accomplishing several objectives intended to back up the single-market efforts. The six objectives of the Single European Act were:

- first, of course, to complete the single market,

- second, to put in place structural policies aimed at helping the poorer EC countries catch up with their richer neighbors,

- third, to establish cooperation on research and technology throughout the Community,

- fourth, to encourage monetary cooperation, and eventually converge to a single European currency,

- fifth, to initiate an EC-wide social policy aimed at harmonizing working conditions across the Community, and improving the dialogue between management and labor,

- sixth, to create a standard environmental policy for all EC nations.

Though the benefits of some of these policies have become surrounded by debate (particularly the social policy), they are intended to complement the single-market effort and are asserted by many top EC officials as being essential to its success. Since the Single European Act was written, the Treaty of Maastricht has fortified many of its objectives by defining explicit plans toward implementing them.

The Philosophy of the White Paper

The White Paper was unlike previous initiatives to harmonize the national markets of the EC in that it was comprehensive in nature. It sought to define a program that would systematically transform the fragmented market into a fully integrated, common market. Its ambition was to inject new focus and enthusiasm into the idea of a single European market, and its underlying purpose was to provide a workable methodology to abolish every rule that caused distorted competition or artificial price differences.

The Paper's philosophy was relatively straight-forward. It was written from the standpoint that *every* barrier had to be removed—that the persistence of even one would invalidate the program. Thus, it began by identifying *all* the offending barriers. Obstructions to free-trade could be found in many forms, ranging from the obvious, such as border patrols, to the more obscure, like differences in intellectual property laws that caused the procedure for obtaining a trademark to vary broadly from one member state to the next. Once the barriers were identified, they were grouped by type into three general categories: physical, technical and fiscal.

Physical barriers, straightforwardly, are the physical obstructions and encumbrances that prevented the free movement of people and goods within the Community. The primary type of physical barrier is, of course, the dreaded border patrols or customs posts that had become situated on every road that crossed a national border throughout Europe.

Technical barriers are those that are caused by differences in specifications or product regulations. Perhaps the most obvious examples of technical barriers are the variety of electrical outlets and plug configurations that can be found throughout the Community. The varying dimensions and shapes of the plugs make it impossible (without an adapter or new plug) to use an appliance universally.

Lastly, fiscal barriers are those obstacles that arise due to different tax rates being charged by the various national governments. The consequences of these differences, and the barriers to free trade caused by them, will be discussed later in this chapter.

These three categories of obstructions are intrinsically linked. Most of the tasks performed at border patrols are caused by technical and fiscal requirements. The White Paper recognized these interrelations. It was aware that simply mandating the removal of offending barriers, such as the border patrols, would not only be virtually impossible—the member states had deeply rooted reasons for requiring them—but would be insufficient to create the desired common market. Instead, the underlying cause of each barrier had to be examined. In each case, the consequences of simply removing the barrier's source was studied. If the outcome was acceptable, the regulation causing the barrier was simply eliminated. When it was not possible to simply do away with an offending rule, an alternative, open-border arrangement was devised.

Physical Barriers—how they were removed.

Of the three categories of barriers, physical barriers are the most obvious to ordinary citizens. Passport controls and immigration checks had become an accepted, albeit disliked, part of traveling in Europe. Abandoning these checks was a priority of the Commission, partly because their removal would help win public support for the single-market program. But, it should be reemphasized that concern for travelers was not the primary reason for eliminating border controls. The true motive was based on the hard, practical fact that keeping the internal border patrols would perpetuate the costs and disadvantages discussed previously.

Border patrols exist for many reasons. One of their primary purposes is to collect taxes and excises on goods traded internationally. As discussed in the next sections, this requirement is a direct consequence of technical and fiscal barriers. By eliminating the technical and fiscal barriers, many functions of the border patrols automatically become unnecessary.

The primary purpose of border patrols that is not related to fiscal or technical matters are those related to national security—checking for illegal immigrants, criminals and terrorists. This requirement was eliminated by increasing security at the EC's external borders, making internal border checks redundant. A similar situation exists in the United States, where the international borders are heavily guarded, but there are no controls at interstate borders.

Additionally, spot checks continue within the EC to check for illegal activity. These spot checks will not necessarily be at borders, but may occur randomly within any member state. Meanwhile, the Community's national police forces are increasing their anti-drug and anti-crime cooperation, raising the Community's ability to fight crime.

These measures, combined with those used to remove the technical and fiscal barriers, were sufficient to enable the EC to open its internal borders. In 1990 representatives from Belgium, France, Germany, Luxembourg and the Netherlands signed documents that gave effect to the Schengen Agreement. This accord, which eliminated border controls for travelers between its five participating countries, was initially undertaken in 1985, but collapsed in 1989 because of the reunification of Germany. When the EC recognized that West Germany was irreversibly dedicated to reunification, the agreement was reinstated, providing an excellent prototype for the larger removal of controls mandated by the single-market program.

Technical Barriers—how they were removed.

Initially, the Community attempted to harmonize national standards by defining new specifications that would replace the member state's existing regulations. This approach, however, was largely unsuccessful. The approval process was complex, and often years were spent on proposals attempting to agree on minute technical details. EC officials became convinced that a better approach had to be adopted, and one was.

The new approach is based on *mutual recognition.* Mutual recognition requires that a product permitted to be sold in one EC member state be accepted in all the member states. Under the mutual recognition approach, member states remain free to maintain their national rules on matters not essential to health and safety—but they must also accept products from other EC countries, even if they are prepared differently and according to other specifications. The European Court of Justice ensures that the member states abide by these requirements.

The mutual recognition approach has enabled products to be sold throughout the Community, letting European consumers choose between domestic products and a host of foreign products. No longer is France allowed to ban artificial sweeteners in soft drinks. Pasta that doesn't comply with the Italian requirement that pasta contain only durum flour can be sold in Italy. Consumers in Spain can buy whiskey that does not meet the Spanish standard that all whiskey be aged for three years and have an alcohol content between 40 and 58 proof. All of which benefit the consumer's right to choice (without sacrificing safety), while simultaneously eliminating the need for border controls to check that imported goods satisfy national requirements.

The EC does still provide some legislation relevant to production and marketing, but only in areas that are considered *essential requirements,* such as human health and safety. These directives define mandatory requirements only as general levels of protection. The specifics are left to be determined by established European standardization bodies (CEN, Cenelec and ETSI), which are more properly suited to do the job. Telecommunications is excepted from the "essential requirements" rule. Though not an essential requirement, there are fairly comprehensive EC standards in the telecommunications industry. These standards are intended to break up the monopolies owned by state telephone companies, and will help Europe remain current in telecommunications technology.

Fiscal Barriers—how they were removed.

As mentioned, a fiscal barrier arises whenever one country charges less tax on a given item than another. This makes the purchase of that item preferable in the country with the lower tax rate, tempting people to buy it there instead of in their home country. Before the single-market program, when consumers bought something outside their own country, they had to declare it upon returning home and pay any applicable taxes on it. All goods that crossed a national border were elaborately documented so that the appropriate taxes and excise duties could be collected. In this system, border patrols were an integral and indispensable part of the system and served two essential fiscal purposes. First, they ensured that the appropriate tax was paid when a cross-border transaction took place (and that the appropriate government received it), and second, they were necessary to counter fraud and tax evasion. The arrival of the common market has required that new methods of accomplishing these functions be found. But before describing the Commission's solution to this problem, some understanding of the traditional European tax system is necessary.

Tax Fundamentals and the Former System in Europe

The European taxation system is considerably different from that of the US. To make any sense out of the EC's newly implemented tax system, some fundamental concepts of taxation must be introduced. First, the difference between a direct tax and an indirect tax. Direct tax refers to taxes taken directly from a company's profits or an individual's income. The "income tax" paid by all workers in the US is the most familiar form of direct tax. Indirect taxes, on the other hand, are those taxes that are included in the price of goods or services. The familiar "sales tax" in the United States is an indirect tax.

The objective of the Commission, regarding tax policy, is to bring about the changes necessary to open up the Community's internal borders—not, as some national politicians have feared, to attempt to force "the perfect taxation system" on the member states. Since different indirect taxation policies cause border patrols, the European Community is involved primarily with indirect taxes. Most matters concerning direct taxation have little relevance to the common market, so rules concerning direct taxation remain at the discretion of the individual national governments.

By far, the most predominant form of indirect tax in the EC is the Value-Added Tax, or VAT. VAT, which was introduced in the Community in 1967, is a type of indirect tax in which tax on a product is paid at each stage of its production, based on the value-added to the raw goods by the manufacturing process. Companies must pay VAT on all supplies needed to manufacture an item, but are effectively reimbursed when they sell the goods. When an item is sold, VAT tax is included in the price of the item. The seller can keep all the collected VAT that he paid out when purchasing the materials needed to manufacture the product. Thus, as the product grows in value, as it passes from one stage of manufacture to the next, the amount of VAT that must be paid to buy it grows accordingly. In the end, only the final consumer bears the burden of the entire tax because he is not reimbursed as those before him were. This sequence of VAT collection, payment and reimbursement is often referred to as the "VAT chain." The figure below gives a simplistic example of how the process works.

The underlying principle in cross-border tax collection is that the tax should be paid by the final consumer and credited to the government of the country where the goods are finally con-

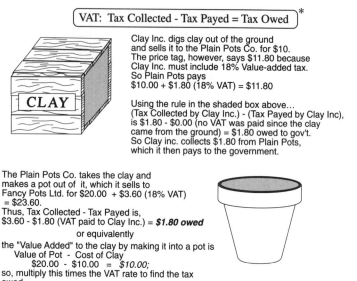

VAT: Tax Collected - Tax Payed = Tax Owed *

Clay Inc. digs clay out of the ground and sells it to the Plain Pots Co. for $10. The price tag, however, says $11.80 because Clay Inc. must include 18% Value-added tax. So Plain Pots pays
$10.00 + $1.80 (18% VAT) = $11.80

Using the rule in the shaded box above...
(Tax Collected by Clay Inc.) - (Tax Payed by Clay Inc), is $1.80 - $0.00 (no VAT was paid since the clay came from the ground) = $1.80 owed to gov't. So Clay inc. collects $1.80 from Plain Pots, which it then pays to the government.

The Plain Pots Co. takes the clay and makes a pot out of it, which it sells to Fancy Pots Ltd. for $20.00 + $3.60 (18% VAT) = $23.60.
Thus, Tax Collected - Tax Payed is,
$3.60 - $1.80 (VAT paid to Clay Inc.) = *$1.80 owed*
or equivalently
the "Value Added" to the clay by making it into a pot is
Value of Pot - Cost of Clay
$20.00 - $10.00 = *$10.00;*
so, multiply this times the VAT rate to find the tax owed...
$10.00 X 18%(VAT) = *$1.80 VAT owed*

plus

Next, Fancy Pots Ltd. takes the plain pot and buys some glaze for $5.00, on which it must pay VAT of .90¢ (18%), for a total cost of $5.90. It then glazes the pot and sells it to the final consumer for $30.00, plus 18% VAT of $5.40, for a total price of $35.40.

Again...
Tax Collected - Tax Payed
$5.40 - [$3.60 + .90¢]
(from consumer) (VAT paid to Plain Pots Co.) (VAT payed on glaze)
= .90¢ VAT owed

Note that only the final consumer ends up actually paying any tax...everyone else is reimbursed when they sell the product.

The VAT (Value-Added Tax) Chain

---

* The cardinal rule of the Value Added Tax system is that the taxes a company owes the government are equal to the taxes it collected from those it sold its products to, minus the taxes it payed when buying the supplies to make the products.

sumed. Thus, if a product is manufactured in Germany and exported to France, the French consumer is expected to pay the tax, not the German manufacturer. Furthermore, because a French consumer is paying the tax, the French treasury should receive the tax revenue, not the German.

The way the traditional system (with border patrols) accomplished this was by imposing VAT tax on imported goods, and reimbursing all paid VAT taxes when a product is exported. For example, when a German automobile manufacturer builds an automobile and then exports it, the German government refunds all the value-added taxes the manufacturer paid when building the car. The French government then taxes the French importer, resulting in the taxes being paid and received correctly.

The problem with this method is that it is dependent on the existence of border controls to document the importation and exportation of goods. Without border controls, the German manufacturer could claim that goods were exported, collect the tax refund from the German government, but never actually export the goods, thereby avoiding the tax. The border control is required to ensure that the goods were really exported. Furthermore, if the border controls were removed without somehow unifying tax treatment in the various nations, large numbers of individuals and traders would go to countries with lower tax rates to buy products, either for their own consumption, or for resale in their home countries at a price that would undercut all competitors. This would disrupt normal market practices, and would prevent governments from collecting some of the tax they are due. Since none of these results are consistent with the goals of the single-market program, it became obvious that if the border controls were to go, an entirely new system of indirect tax collection would need to be devised. This has proven to be one of the single market's most difficult challenges because the member states' tax policies vary tremendously, yet EC proposals concerning taxation require unanimous approval.

Despite the difficulties, the EC was able to adopt a new tax system that has enabled the Community's internal border controls to be removed. The system emerged only after heavy negotiation, and was the result of several successive rounds of Commission proposals being modified by the Council. It is, alas, only a transitional system that must be replaced by January 1997, and it is not perfect. But in fairness, and in view of the Commission's primary goal, it has indeed eliminated the necessity of border controls for tax collection purposes.

Toward a New Tax System—the Commission's First Proposal

The outcome the Commission desires, regarding tax harmonization, is that the fiscal system of the single market work the same as the system of an individual member state. In other words, companies should be able to regard export sales exactly the same as domestic sales. Any difference between the two stifles the proper operation of the single market. When a company makes a domestic sale it charges the buyer VAT and is able to reclaim the VAT it paid while manufacturing the item. For an export sale, the company must undertake a different procedure by which VAT is refunded. Ideally, exporters would charge the same VAT rate on sales for exports as for domestic transactions, and importers would reclaim that as input tax, just as they would for domestic purchases. Thus all VAT collection would occur in the product's *country of origin.*

The Commission's initial attempt to harmonize EC indirect taxes was a proposal that defined two VAT rate bands as shown in the figure on the next page. The bands would apply to different categories of products and the member states would be able set their VAT rates at any level within the bands. The bands proposed were 14% to 20% as the standard rate, and 4% to 9% as the reduced rate. The reduced rate was intended to be used for certain categories of items such as food or other essentials, and the standard rate for everything else (although many member states also were accustomed to using a third, increased rate that applied to luxury goods, such as yachts or Ferraris).

The two-band system was based on the idea that it is possible to have different tax rates from nation to nation and still avoid upsetting trade, as long as the differences are small. The United States attests to this argument. State-to-state differences in tax rates exist as high as 6%, even among bordering states, and no significant disruption of trade has been felt.

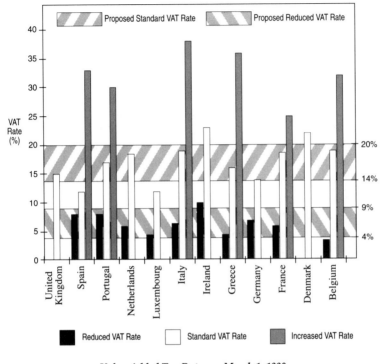

**Value-Added Tax Rates on March 1, 1990
and Proposed Harmonized Rates**

But the EC's proposed two-band system was met with a large variety of opposition from member states. Denmark and Ireland were concerned that rates proposed by the bands were too low, and the loss of revenue would be detrimental. Luxembourg felt that they were too high, and that increasing their standard VAT rate to the EC mandated level would cause major price increases and lead to business closures and unemployment. The UK was concerned that there was no provision for "zero-rating," or charging no VAT on certain items, as it had become accustomed to with children's clothing and other social necessities. Overall, consensus was not even closely achieved, and although the Council agreed to the proposal *in principal*, they felt that it would be impossible to implement by the December 31, 1992, deadline.

Instead, the Council said it would agree to a transitional plan that allowed the removal of fiscal barriers, but maintained taxation in the *country of destination* (as had always been the case).

The Accepted Transitional Tax System

The Commission was disappointed that the member states would not accept the two-band VAT proposal, but to maintain the prime objective of abolishing tax related border checks, they presented a transitional system with a more flexible approach. The transitional system was unanimously accepted by the Council on June 24, 1991. Its acceptance made it possible to abolish all border procedures related to the movement of goods beginning on January 1, 1993.

The transitional system sets a minimum VAT rate of 15%, with an optional 5% reduced rate. Member states are free to choose their rate(s) above this minimum, and may apply one or two reduced rates not lower than 5%. Existing rates below 5% and zero-rated items are allowed to remain in place. All the higher rates of VAT levied on luxury goods have been abolished. To eliminate the border controls two things have occurred. For companies, verification that a product has been exported is accomplished by a declaration from both the exporter and importer. Individuals are free to buy anything they desire in other member states (paying VAT there) and return home with those purchases without formalities. The purchases, however, must be for their personal consumption.

With the exception of private vehicles (cars and motorcycles) the transitional agreement has eliminated restrictions on purchases in other countries. Excise duties on tobacco, alcoholic beverages, and oil products such as gasoline, which varied widely before the common market program, have also been harmonized. Minimum rates on beer, wine, cigarettes and oil products have been agreed on, and came into force on January 1, 1993. Although some member states have had to raise their excise duties and others lower theirs, the overall amount of revenue collected remains unchanged because the new EC-rates are an unweighted average of the member states previous rates.

There are special rules, however, that apply to cars and mail-order sales. For cars, VAT is charged at the rate of the country where the vehicle will be registered, regardless of where it is purchased. For mail-order products, VAT must be paid at the rate of the country of destination. The special rules for automobiles are one of the major shortcomings of the common market. Varying VAT rates within the EC can lead to price differences as large as 200% on the same type of car.

The transitional arrangement is less than the ideal initially hoped for by the Commission. Companies must still make a distinction between a domestic sale and an export sale. Taxes are still collected in the country of destination, and exporters are still reimbursed by their governments. This, however, was made necessary by the original wide disparities between the member states and it won't last forever. The Council has already agreed that the transitional system must be replaced by a system in which all VAT taxes are collected in the country of origin by December 31, 1996.

Additional tax matters

Double taxation is a phenomenon that arises when the profits of a company's foreign branches are taxed once in the foreign country, and then again when the profits are distributed as dividends in the company's home country. Such a practice is obviously damaging to free-trade and should not occur in any properly operating free market. Before the common market, double taxation created "invisible" barriers in the EC that effectively kept companies from cooperating as they would in a unified market. Mergers between firms established in different member states often failed due to the negative effects of double taxation.

Today, sufficient legislation has been passed by the Council to greatly reduce the risk of this type of barrier. As the common market matures, additional legislation will be implemented whenever required to assure that firms operating in two or more EC countries do not have a tax disadvantage compared to those operating in only one country. Differences between the member states' tax systems are allowed, but only to the extent that they do not adversely affect the investment behavior of firms, or competition.

Progress Achieved by the Single-Market Program

Now that the single-market program has officially opened, the effect of the EC's ambitious plan to transform itself into one market with 340 million free-spending consumers can be appraised. Overall, the reforms have been completed with remarkable success. Though debate rages over the future goals of the Community, and whether monetary, social and political union should be sought, virtually all Europeans can agree on the single-market concept. The very prospect of the Single Market inspires many Europeans and now, EC officials can boast of spectacular achievements toward liberalizing the European marketplace.

Many of the single-market program's accomplishments, however, have been achieved through compromise. Hundreds of small and large compromises were made in the run-up to 1992. As a result, some of the new rules will not become effective until the end of 1993, or even later. Concessions and special rules have been made for poorer countries giving them time to catch up with their more developed neighbors. For example, the rules on free movement of goods do not take effect in Spain or Portugal until 1995. A few of the program's original concepts have been dropped altogether. A proposal to create a European company statute has been pushed aside because Germany wants European companies to provide worker representation on their boards of directors, but Britain and five other member states refuse to accept this idea.

In spite of a few shortcomings, the Single European Market is the EC's most outstanding accomplishment to date. It is part of a global trend toward free trade, and has eliminated many unnecessary restrictions in Europe while leaving regional flavors and traditions intact.

Border Checks Largely Eliminated

The removal of physical border controls was one of the most successful endeavors of the 1992 program. Border controls no longer exist for individual travelers within the EC, and trucks may roll across international borders hassle free (except in Spain and Portugal who are waiting until 1995). With the exception of certain dangerous substances such as explosives or radioactive material, anyone can import or export anything they desire.

The United Kingdom remains the only major stumbling block to the idea of completely open borders. British authorities steadfastly refuse to outlaw border checks as a part of the common-market program, saying they are a necessary precaution for an island nation such as themselves. They insist that travelers must be screened to check for drug runners, illegal immigrants and disease bearing plants and animals at their point of arrival: airports, ferry terminals and the new channel tunnel. The EC is hoping to eventually convince the UK that increased security at the EC's external borders is a sufficient safeguard against terrorist threats, and that the British should, therefore, eliminate the passport controls at their borders.

People Free to Live and Work Abroad—Credentials Universal

Before the common market, people were often unable to change the country in which they practiced their profession due to differences in required qualifications. A pharmacist in one country may not have been qualified as a pharmacist in another.

Prior to the Single European Act, the Community attempted to specifically define the qualifications necessary to practice a given profession. Every member state had to agree on these qualifications, and the negotiations regarding each profession were normally long and complex. For example, the directives that were finally issued defining the qualifications of an EC-certified architect took 17 years. The most progress, using this approach, was achieved in the medical field. Doctors, nurses, dentists and veterinarians all had their basic training requirements harmonized and were thus able to practice freely anywhere within the EC. They were given what the Community calls the "right of establishment," which, in essence, is the right to practice in all EC countries.

For many professions, however, the harmonized qualifications necessary to grant "right of establishment" were never achieved. Facing the impossibly slow negotiations that would result from harmonizing the qualifications of every type of profession was not a real option for the 1992 program. Yet, establishing the free movement of people was one of the program's fundamental goals. To overcome this dilemma the EC used the same approach that it used for products—the mutual recognition approach.

A directive was passed allowing a person who is qualified as a professional in one member state to be given the same recognition in any member state. All higher education qualifications from any accredited institution within the EC are now valid throughout the Community. Specific education policies remain national responsibilities, but the member states are obliged to accept credentials from other EC countries. This general rule applies in virtually all cases. It has enabled EC professionals to work throughout the Community and is subject only to limited additional requirements, such as a period of supervised practice before being given full credentials in a new country.

Free movement of Capital—Banks, Insurance and Investments

Banks   The passage of the 1992 deadline ushered in a new era in banking in which banks in one member state were, for the first time, given the right to freely market their services in other member states. This right also allows them to open branches anywhere in the EC if they so desire. The new rules make EC banks even freer than those in the United States; EC banks are now permitted to grow into Europe-wide-super banks that offer all the traditional banking services and can also sell insurance and underwrite securities. Free movement of capital has made it possible to open a bank account anywhere in the EC and to transfer unlimited funds from country to country.

EC banks, along with other investment companies, will be allowed to join stock exchanges outside their home country beginning in 1995. In Belgium, France and Italy, this will be permitted starting in 1996, while Spanish, Greek and Portuguese banks will need to wait until 1999.

Insurance   The broad emancipation from the old ways of doing business for the insurance industry doesn't come until mid 1994. Currently, insurance companies must follow twelve widely varying sets of national regulations that explicitly dictate how they can run their business. New rules put in place by the single-market program will put an end to this by mid 1994. In 1994, an insurance company will be able to operate in all twelve national markets, but will be required to follow only one set of regulations—those of its home country. If excessively regulated countries do not reform their rules, they will risk loosing valuable insurance-industry companies to EC countries with less stringent requirements. This threat will effectively force member states to deregulate their insurance industries and will likely lead to an increased variety of insurance products and more competitive pricing.

<u>Investment services</u>   The process of opening up investment services will take place from 1995 to 1999. Presently, investment companies in the Community may open offices in another EC member state only by establishing a heavily capitalized subsidiary there. Even then, the subsidiary has no guarantee of success. Foreign firms are often barred from local stock exchanges, making it impossible for a foreign firm to underwrite securities for companies outside its home market. In France, investment firms are protected by a monopoly dating from the Napoleonic era, which channels all securities business through one of 57 existing brokerage houses.

These limitations make it more difficult for new or expanding enterprises to seek financing and reduce opportunities for investors. To correct this situation, the single-market program introduced several new directives that were designed to loosen controls on investment activity. As a result, EC banks and investment firms will be able to establish branches anywhere within the Community beginning in 1995, without being required to expend extraordinary amounts of capital to do so. They will be allowed to join local stock exchanges and will be able to underwrite securities for any EC company. These measures will enable investors to choose investments from anywhere within the Community, and entrepreneurs will be able to seek financing from any EC bank or brokerage house.

Trouble Spots within the Single-Market Program

In spite of all the progress that has been achieved, the December 31, 1992, deadline did not quite usher in an era in which conducting business between Spain and Britain is as hassle free as it is between Oregon and California. Certain obstacles remain. Some of them are simply stubborn, but will in time be abolished. Others will likely persist, in one form or another, indefinitely.

The obvious disadvantages of not having a common currency will remain until a common currency is adopted—an event not likely until 1997 at the earliest, and probably not before the turn of the century. There are obstacles caused by the Community's many languages, cultures, traditions and historical experiences that are very real and very slow to disappear. EC law may mandate that public authorities receive bids for public-works contracts from throughout the Community, but it cannot do away with the many informal processes that frequently result in contracts being awarded locally. Relief from this type of barrier can only occur naturally over time as Europeans become more accustomed to working with each other.

Overall, though, the 1992 program was outstandingly successful. It has introduced the EC to the advantages of cross-border business and has provided options for its citizens and workers that were altogether unavailable a short time ago. It will make Europe more competitive, give more choice to its consumers and serve as the necessary platform to launch Europe into the next century.

6

European Monetary Union

We are not merging States, we are uniting men.

–Jean Monnet, EC Founding Father

Most large EC companies ardently support efforts to replace the Community's twelve national currencies with one common currency. Though the single market has made cross-border transactions in Europe easier than ever before, it has not released firms from the inconveniences of exchange rates. All exporting EC companies must still contend with the problems and uncertainties caused by constantly shifting inter-Community currency valuations, and envious eyes are cast toward the United States where an enormous market is complemented by the always accepted, stable dollar.

European Monetary Union (EMU), the catchall title for monetary integration efforts in the Community, is presently the heart of the unification struggle. With the majority of the single market reforms now successfully implemented, it is the next logical step. EMU's ultimate goal is to irrevocably fix the exchange rates between the twelve national currencies and then merge them into one common currency. This, however, is proving to be a very difficult task.

The blueprint for economic and monetary union has evolved over many years. Previously abandoned efforts and a variety of studies and reports have all influenced the present approach. In 1988, the European Council instructed a committee chaired by Commission President Jacques Delors to suggest a specific methodology toward achieving economic and monetary union. After 10 months of effort, the Delors committee presented its findings in a report entitled "Report on economic and monetary union in the European Community." The report detailed, in three stages, a procedure to bring about a single currency. It also pointed out that the Treaty of Rome did not have the capacity for such an objective, thereby making a treaty change mandatory (followed by the necessary changes in national laws) if monetary union was to become a reality.

In 1991, the methodology proposed by the Delors Report, as well as the necessary changes to the Community's treaties, became the heart of the now familiar Treaty of Maastricht. The treaty, which is formally known as the *Treaty on European Union,* has now been ratified by all twelve member nations. Its acceptance, however, did not come easily. During the bruising journey through the member nation's acceptance procedures, it became apparent that some problems exist in the treaty's monetary-union scheme. A primary weakness is its reliance on the member states' ability to keep the value of their currencies within narrow trading ranges. As will be discussed shortly, this requirement has already broken down, ensuring that when and if monetary unification is achieved, it will have been attained via some variation of the Treaty's present plan. Though revision seems inescapable, the Treaty of Maastricht is currently the center of efforts to unify European monetary policy. It serves as a hub for debate and negotiation, and it is a necessary stepping stone toward further progress. Monetary union is a complex task, particularly in an organization as economically and culturally diverse as the European Community. The fact that difficulties are being encountered during its development should not come as a surprise.

The ideas in the Maastricht Treaty, including monetary union, are regarded with varying degrees of enthusiasm. For proponents of a unified Europe, the Maastricht treaty represents the welcome bridge toward a fully integrated Europe, which would evolve to function much like the United States. On the other end of the spectrum, however, to those with more conservative views concerning European cooperation, Maastricht represents an absolute limit to what should be accomplished in terms of central control and loss of independent national decision making and is thus viewed with controversy and skepticism. But why is economic and monetary union being sought at all and why is it considered controversial? There are both economic and political answers to these questions, and to fully understand the implications of EMU, both must be examined.

There are several economic reasons to pursue monetary union—most of them coming from the voice of European business. First, businesses find EMU appealing because the ability to conduct transactions with only one currency would eliminate the present risks and costs associated with multiple currencies. Eliminating exchange rates would remove the risk an exporting company must presently take of being forced to reduce its profit margins due to unexpected currency devaluations. It would also eliminate currency conversion costs. EMU supporters argue that this would enable European companies to finally cease worrying about currency valuations and projections, enabling them to concentrate on more important aspects of business (like competition from abroad). Second, it is hoped that EMU would help to impose monetary discipline on the entire Community similar to that of the German Bundesbank. The Bundesbank's strict rules have enabled Germany to become Europe's economic powerhouse and it is thought that the adoption of its policies by the other member states would eventually create an environment of low inflation and price stability throughout the Community. A third reason, cited by EMU fans, to embrace a common currency is that financial reports and other money related documents would become uniform, thereby making the market more efficient and making comparison of companies easier and more coherent.

In addition to economic incentives, there are some powerful political reasons why monetary harmonization in Europe is being encouraged. One fundamental and obvious reason for politically embracing EMU is simply that business wants it. Since European business represents a powerful political lobbying force, good public relations dictate that politicians be influenced by it. But beyond this, there are some purely political arguments for coveting EMU that have little to do with pressure from European business, and are intricately linked with the 1992 single-market program.

Before the single market, businesses in Europe had little control over gains and losses associated with currency fluctuations. There were laws that effectively forced them to conduct transactions in their country's currency, regardless of its value against other currencies. Thus, companies in countries with unstable currencies were forced to brave the stormy waters of the international currency market whenever they wished to import or export goods. In the newly created free market, brought about by the

Single European Act, capital is allowed to flow freely across national borders, bringing new opportunities to businesses which were previously forced to contend with an unstable currency. For example, if an Italian businessman becomes fed up with the roller-coaster ride associated with the value of the lira, making it difficult for him to assess his capital requirements, he could simply remove all his transaction operations from Italy and conduct them in Germany or Belgium or anywhere else in the EC where the currency is more stable. The phenomenon of conducting transactions in a foreign currency, to avoid a domestic currency's undesirable characteristics, is known as currency flight. Currency flight was previously illegal and businesses caught doing it were subject to stiff penalties. Under a truly free market, however, as the EC wants its internal market to be, currency flight cannot be outlawed. To take the example even further, if a government implemented policies that made its currency particularly unstable, citizens would begin to deposit their money into accounts denominated in more stable currencies. This would greatly decrease a government's ability to influence its economy through interest rate adjustments and other traditional controls. Thus, EMU is desirable from a political point of view because in a monetarily united Europe there would be no benefit from currency flight, thereby enabling governments to retain a greater degree of control over their economies than would be possible without EMU. Short of reverting to the days of currency controls—a move that would be directly opposite the spirit of the single market—EMU is seen as the best way to ensure that EC national governments operating in the post 1992 environment can exert some real influence on their economies.

The European Monetary System

Before discussing the Treaty of Maastricht's plan to achieve a European monetary union, it is necessary to describe the history and workings of current monetary controls in the EC. In the late 1960s, increasing monetary instability in Europe (widely fluctuating exchange rates) caused politicians to become concerned about the viability of some of the reforms put in place by the European Economic Community. France, in particular, was worried that a decrease in the value of the French franc would deteriorate the agricultural subsidies it received from the Community, putting French national development plans in jeopardy. In 1969, two studies, known as the Barre Reports, released additional evidence that the monetary policies of the member states were threatening the customs union. In response to these concerns, the reports offered a plan calling for the establishment of monetary coordination between the EC countries. Concerned by the conclusion of the Barre reports, the Council of Ministers agreed at a 1969 Hague summit to study ways to implement closer monetary cooperation.

Although the benefits varied from one member state to the next, each member state stood to gain something from the establishment of a monetary union. Not surprisingly, though, when the finance ministers of the six EC countries met later, there were wide differences of opinion regarding how best to achieve monetary union, and no conclusions were reached. Instead, it was decided that a study group should be established to investigate the alternatives and then arrive at a specific, usable plan.

A group was assembled for this purpose under the chairmanship of M. Pierre Werner, the prime minister of Luxembourg. In 1970, it released a report that has become the primary model for European monetary integration. Known as the Werner Report, the study developed many of the concepts for monetary harmonization that are being used today. The Werner Report specifically called for the creation of a European currency unit and the gradual narrowing of exchange-rate fluctuations, eventually leading to fixed rates.[8] This led to the implementation of a system of exchange-rate controls known as the "snake."

The "snake" was implemented in 1972 by the original EC member states—the United Kingdom, Ireland, Denmark and Norway later participated in it as well. The UK withdrew only two months after it joined the scheme and Italy and France also forsook the arrangement. The "snake" didn't work very well. Its

---

8. Fixed exchange rates mean, for example, that 1 British pound might be worth exactly 2.49 German marks. Any day. Anytime. Anywhere. Currently, EC currencies may vary in value with respect to one another.

strengths were only in keeping the exchange rates of currencies in sync that were unlikely to deviate anyway. It did, however, highlight the difficulty of merging the currencies of countries with vastly different economies and economic policies. A political declaration is far from sufficient to keep currencies in alignment—corresponding economic policies must also be put into place before any exchange-rate controls can have a chance of success. Despite its insights, most attempts to implement the steps specified by the Werner plan failed. They would have to wait nine years for the establishment of the European Monetary System to be implemented more successfully.

Even though the EC failed to properly implement the ideas in the Werner Report, the search for monetary harmonization, within the Community, remained important. The EC nations trade vigorously among themselves, and revenue accrued from cross-border trade accounts for a large percentage of each nation's gross national product (half of all EC trade is internal). Because of this dependency upon sales from across their respective borders, each EC member nation is very sensitive to the others' economic policies—particularly monetary and fiscal policies, which influence currency exchange rates and international trade.

In 1972, the Commission called to restore efforts toward achieving European monetary union. The arrangements that subsequently developed are called the European Monetary System (EMS).

The European Monetary System (EMS) is one of common, international, financial structures that were adopted by the member states in 1979. It has three essential elements: the Exchange Rate Mechanism (ERM), which places limits on the value of the various EC national currencies; the European Currency Unit (ECU), the unit of currency that the EC hopes will one day replace the national currencies; and the European Monetary Cooperation Fund, which acts as a source of loans for the member states' Central Banks, and as a clearing house (an institution that settles mutual indebtedness between organizations).

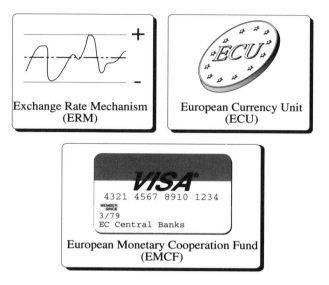

The Elements of the European Monetary System (EMS)

The ECU

The European Currency Unit, or ECU, is the official currency of the European Community. Currently, one ECU is worth approximately $1.13.[9] The ECU has not replaced any of the member states' national currencies yet, and in fact could not because so far no official ECU coins have been minted or bills printed. The Community's accounting is performed using ECUs, however, and loans and bonds are often denominated in ECUs both by governments and companies. Presently, the ECU is a currency in name only. It serves as a unit of account in which bank balances can be maintained, loans made and bills paid, but no physical ECUs exist yet. The ECU presently stands as an alternative to the individual national currencies, rather than replacing them. The ultimate goal of monetary union is, of course, to replace the individual national currencies with the ECU.

The ECU was first introduced in 1973. It is made up of "a basket" of national currencies, that is, its value is determined by

---

9.   Exchange rate on July 12, 1993 as quoted by the *Wall Street Journal Europe*.

specific amounts of member states' currencies—the more economically important having a larger share of the composition. The percentage share of each of the member states' currencies for 1990 is shown by the following figure.

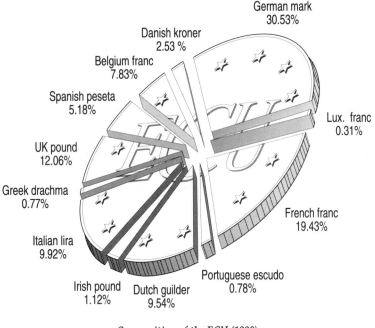

Composition of the ECU (1990);
Percentage Share of Each Currency

Presently, it is possible to open a bank account denominated in ECUs, pay with ECU checks or buy ECU bonds. Its exchange rate with the other major currencies of the world is calculated and published daily. The ECU is popular for borrowing or lending because it is more stable than other currencies. Since it is an average of many countries' funds, it tends to even out the fluctuations that affect individual currencies. This stability has helped make it the sixth most popular unit in the world for denominating international loans, behind the dollar, yen, Swiss franc, pound sterling, and German mark.

Although no ECU bills or coins exist yet, the currency still serves several important functions. It is the benchmark for fixing the central rates on which the permissible fluctuations of the Exchange Rate Mechanism are based. It constitutes the point of reference for an early warning system designed to induce governments to take economic policy measures even before the permissible fluctuation margins have been reached. It is the denominator for payment transactions between central banks and settlements resulting from purchases and sales in support of exchange rates, and it is the denominator for Community balance-of-payments' assistance to member states in economic difficulties.[10]

The ECU should not be confused with the ancient French coin, the Ecu (eh-koo). The ECU was not named after the French coin and the German government has publicly denounced the notion that it was. Many people, though, even EC officials, still pronounce the acronym *E-C-U* as *eh-koo.*

The Exchange Rate Mechanism

Similar to its predecessor the "snake," the European Monetary System (EMS) strives to force member countries to maintain the value of their currency within a narrow range of fluctuation in relation to the other EMS currencies. This is accomplished through an arrangement called the Exchange Rate Mechanism, or ERM. The ERM sets the base exchange rates for each currency, and allows them to deviate only within a defined band of values (e.g., the French franc traded between 0.28 and 0.30 German marks under early 1992 ERM guidelines). In addition to limiting the amount a currency may move relative to other EMS currencies, limits are placed on the amount a currency may move from its base exchange rate with the European Currency Unit (ECU). This percentage varies depending upon a currency's relative importance in calculating the value of the ECU (see the figure on previous page). The more important currencies are allowed to fluctuate less than those of smaller significance. An important difference between the EMS and the earlier "snake" is that it imposes less stringent restrictions on participating currencies and allows less

---

10. European File Series, 1991, *The ECU,* Luxembourg: Office of the Official Publications of the European Communities.

developed countries more leeway. Greece and Portugal are considered only provisional members of the EMS and are subject to looser controls than the other EC countries. They are expected to become full EMS members when their economies mature sufficiently.

The Exchange Rate Mechanism's band of fluctuation is very similar to, albeit broader than, that of the "snake" of the 1970s. As was true with the "snake," an EMS member country whose currency deviates outside the EMS's limits must take whatever action necessary to realign its currency. The organization responsible for this intervention is that particular country's national central bank, which is expected to intervene in the currency markets to whatever degree necessary to keep its nation's currency in line. There are two fundamental actions used by the national central banks to realign currencies when their values begin to wander outside the specified EMS range. If a currency is becoming undervalued by EMS guidelines, the central banks buy the weak currency, which tends to prop up its price. If a currency becomes too highly priced, the central bank(s) sell it on the international foreign exchange markets to lower its price. Additionally, a central bank may influence the value of its currency by adjusting interest rates. If a country has interest rates that are perceived as high, foreign traders clamor to buy that country's currency and deposit it there to take advantage of the high interest rate. The action of the foreign traders swapping their money for that of a given country, causes the value of the country's currency to rise.

When it is necessary for a central bank to intervene in the currency markets and buy its currency, it must have constant access to sufficient money to do so. The EC has made provisions to provide national central banks unlimited credit for this purpose. The credit is established through a multinational fund called the European Monetary Cooperation Fund (EMCF), which maintains its funds in ECUs. The EMCF is financed by the Community's members. Each member states' Central Bank deposits 20% of its gold and foreign exchange reserves with the Fund. This pool of assets is available for short-term loans, denominated in ECUs, for currency market intervention when necessary. Loans to a central bank from the EMCF are to be paid back within 45 days, although a three month extension may be arranged.

The EMU Plan as Defined by the Treaty of Maastricht

As stated at the beginning of this chapter, monetary evolution in the EC is currently wrapped up with the fate of the Maastricht treaty. EC leaders hurriedly put together this 311-page document in Maastricht, Netherlands, over a weekend in December 1991. It was completed without any outside consultation and is a complicated document that was not written to be read and understood by the general public. The failure of the Maastricht architects to educate the European public on the goals of the treaty has become one of its greatest weaknesses. Understandably, people would rather support no change than support a change they don't understand. This is one of the primary reasons voters in Denmark rejected the treaty in June, 1992. In 1993, Denmark accepted the Maastricht Treaty in a second referendum, but only after being given the ability to opt out of the treaty's provisions for a common currency and a common military.

The Treaty of Maastricht is composed of two primary parts: one dealing with political union, the other with economic and monetary union. Its most precise and rigid passages are those devoted to Economic and Monetary Union. The Treaty, assuming it survives the ratification process, will provide the necessary amendments to the Treaty of Rome to enable economic and monetary union to become a reality. It will make the creation of a single currency inevitable by January 1, 1999—possibly sooner. A large portion of the treaty is composed of an explanation of how the Community should go about achieving economic and monetary union. It breaks the process into three stages.

The first stage is to formally begin when the treaty is ratified; but, in actuality, it has already begun. It sets in motion the fundamental heart of monetary union, that being the technical process of convergence. Presently, economic indicators between the member states vary broadly. The plan, as set out in the treaty, is to take the appropriate actions to make these differences vanish. In each member state, economic indicators such as inflation, interest rates, exchange fluctuations, budget and public sector deficits should begin to correlate with each other and eventually converge with those of the best performing economies.

If success is attained, it should be straight forward to continue to reduce exchange rate fluctuations until they reach zero, fix the exchange rates, and then replace the individual currencies with one: the ECU. The policies concerning EMU are modeled after those of Germany, who proudly possesses the strong, stable, anti-inflationary Deutsche mark (DM), and it is hoped that the ECU will inherit these characteristics.

At the center of the plans laid out for economic union is an independent central bank, the European Central Bank (ECB), which is also modeled after Germany's ironclad Bundesbank. The ECB will become an influential part of a European System of Central Banks (ESCB). The ESCB will be composed of the ECB and all the central banks from the member states. The primary objective of the ESCB will be to maintain price stability within the community, and strict economic discipline will be required by all participating member states. Additionally, each member state has devoted itself to avoiding excessive budgetary deficits.

Stage I

As called for in the treaty, each national government must begin to implement programs and policies to achieve convergence, and the heads of state, for each member nation, must commit themselves to regard their nation's individual economic policy as both pertinent and as a matter of concern to all members of the EC. The Council of Ministers (specifically the Finance Ministry) is responsible for monitoring the economies of the member nations and reporting any suspect deviation in economic policies or performance. The Council will intervene if "national economic policies are inconsistent with the guidelines or present a risk to EMU."[11] When a deviation is noted by the Council, the offending nation is reprimanded and told how to correct its policy. If a nation has financial difficulties beyond its control, including natural disasters, sources of financial assistance are made available.

---

11. Excerpt from: *Treaty on European Union* (Maastricht, Netherlands: December, 1991).

Additionally, under the Treaty of Maastricht's guidelines, the Commission is responsible for diligently monitoring the government debt levels of the member states. If the accepted level of debt is surpassed, the Commission informs the Council of Ministers. The Finance Ministers of the Council can then require that remedial action be taken. Failure by a member state to comply with these demands will prompt stern and mounting sanctions. The European Investment Bank may "reconsider its lending policy toward the offending country."[12] Additionally, the Community may demand that the offending country "make a non-interest bearing deposit of an appropriate size with the Community until the excessive deficit has been corrected."[13] This is essentially forcing the offender to make an interest free loan to the Community. Finally, the Council may impose fines when deemed necessary. Decisions to impose these punitive measures must come from a two-thirds vote by the Commission, excluding the votes of the offending country's representative(s).

Stage II

Stage II is to begin January 1, 1994. By this time the independence of the national central banks should be in place—leading the way for a new political organization, the European Monetary Institute (EMI), to be established. The EMI will be directed and managed by a Council consisting of the Governors of the national central banks and presided over by a president appointed by national consensus. It will hold as its central tasks:

- the strengthening of cooperation between the national central banks,

- the coordination of monetary policies,

- the facilitation of the use of the ECU and the oversight of the ECU clearing system,

- and the overall monitoring of the European Monetary System.

12., 13.   Excerpt from: *Treaty on European Union* (Maastricht, Netherlands: December, 1991).

The European Council is to be kept informed regarding community progress toward convergence by both the newly founded EMI and the Commission. On December 31, 1996, the European Council must decide whether a majority of the member states meet the convergence criteria. Four factors will be looked at: inflation, budget deficit, interest rates and exchange rates. If it is decided that indeed the majority does meet the minimum criteria, and that it is probable that they will be able to maintain the achieved levels, the Community may set a date to move to Stage III of EMU. If a date is not determined by the end of 1997, the European System of Central Banks must be established regardless by July 1, 1998. Stage III would then begin on January 1, 1999. Only those states who have qualified for the adoption of the common currency will be included in Stage III; those not qualifying will be termed "member states with a derogation" and will give up certain rights. The "member states with a derogation" will be reviewed at least once every two years, or more frequently at their request, for fulfillment of the convergence criteria, and will be admitted into the system when qualified.

Stage III

When Stage III begins, the conversion rates between the various currencies will be irrevocably fixed. National currencies will be exchanged for ECUs and the ECU will become a full fledged currency in its own right. When a "member state with a derogation" has achieved the convergence criteria, their derogation status will be "abrogated" (removed) and the Council will determine a conversion rate at which they may replace their currency with ECUs. As of the first day of Stage III, the European Central Bank will replace the European Monetary Institute, which will go into liquidation. The European Central Bank (ECB) will enjoy absolute independence. It will not be bound by instructions from anyone, whether it be the EC institutions, governments or any other body. All monetary authority will be transferred from the individual national governments to the Community, and the rules and procedures established by the EC in the budgetary and macroeconomic domain will be binding on the member state governments.

Recent Changes in the Exchange Rate Mechanism

The schedule laid out by the Maastricht Treaty was dealt a blow in August 1993, when the EC's finance ministers and central bank governors made a drastic change to the European Monetary System. Under extreme duress, they "temporarily" increased the amount that their currencies may fluctuate against each other. The allowed fluctuation range was boosted from ±2.25% to ±15.00%, except for the relationship between the German mark and the Dutch guilder, which remained unchanged. This move greatly weakened the strength of the EMS and placed the Maastricht Treaty's timetable for monetary union in jeopardy. The change was necessary to halt massive speculative pressure from the world's currency markets, and was considered by many to be a major blow to European Unity. But in many ways, it was the EMS's own policies that invited currency traders to speculate, suggesting that there may be a basic flaw in the EC's approach to monetary union. To better understand the nature of the problems that exist within the European Monetary System, and to gain insight into possible methods of alleviating them, it is helpful to examine the events that led up to the August 1993 decision.

The fundamental principle of the EMS is the idea that rigid adherence to fixed-exchange rates would force member states to adopt common economic policies. This, it was hoped, would eventually lead to full monetary unification and a common currency. The principle has merit, and throughout the 1980s the EMS functioned largely as its founders expected. The problem with the EMS's reasoning is that it depends on the member state's economies having, at least broadly, similar characteristics. The theory begins to break down when the economies in question have fundamentally different needs.

The difficulty revolves around interest rates and their effect on an economy. Central banks use interest rates as a primary economic tool to influence the value of currencies. High interest rates tend to attract capital, thus increasing the value of a currency. Similarly, low interest rates decrease a currency's exchange value. But besides affecting currency valuation, interest rates are also one of the most important tools to stimulate or repress an economy. A country in a recession desires low interest so that money is readily available for investment and growth, while a central bank wishing to combat inflation and slow an economy will generally raise interest rates. The flaws in the ERM began to appear when the interest-rate needs mandated by the ERM began to conflict with those necessary to keep the EC's national economies healthy.

By virtue of its size and high level of industrialization, Germany is the dominant economy in Europe. Though the ERM was designed to align Europe's economic and monetary systems, in reality its affect was to link the other eleven countries to German economic policy. This in itself is not a problem. Germany's economic philosophy was, and is, simple and sound—no inflation, period. In fact, the European ties to Germany were often seen as a positive, with supporters saying the Teutonic discipline of the German central bankers would help other EC countries improve their economies. Problems began to arise, however, when Germany experienced a once-in-a-lifetime event that made the needs of the German economy very different than those of the other EC member states—reunification. Though not known at the time, the fall of the Berlin Wall and the reunification with East Germany would later throw the European Monetary System into chaos.

The terms of reunification were generous, and as West Germany made the massive investments necessary to bring their new countrymen's living standards up to par with their own, the costs became astronomical. The ensuing demand for goods and capital to rebuild East Germany's ruined economy was enormous. German money growth expanded explosively, and inflation began to appear. The Bundesbank, Germany's adamantly independent central bank, dutifully began to tighten monetary policy and increase interest rates to counteract inflationary pressure. But with their currencies tied to the German mark, the other EC member states were also forced to raise interest rates to maintain the value of their currencies. The problem with this was that, unlike Germany who was booming due to the demands of reunification, many other EC nations were caught in deep recessions.

By 1992, two years of extremely tight money had helped Germany slow its economic boom. But by forcing the rest of the EC nations to adopt harmfully high interest rates, it further weakened many other EC country's already recessionary economies. The currency markets became frenzied as speculators bet that the artificially supported currencies would be unable to maintain their values. On September 16, 1992, the United Kingdom, Italy and Spain relented to market forces and sharply devalued their currencies after weeks of chaotic trading in the European financial markets. Europeans called it "Black Wednesday." Massive intervention by central banks, all over the world, were unable to stop the flow of capital away from the EC countries which were suffering from weak economies and recessionary conditions. The central banks of England and Italy gave up the struggle and quit the ERM indefinitely to pursue economic policies focused on their own needs rather than those of Germany.

After "Black Wednesday" currency markets calmed down for a while, but this repose was short lived because many disparities still existed and interest rates were still too high in several EC countries. In August 1993, after the Bundesbank disappointed markets by refusing to lower a key interest rate, sufficient pressure returned to force the EC to surrender and widen the ERM's trading bands.

At the time this book went to press, the allowed fluctuation in the ERM was still ±15%, and EC leaders were frantically searching for methods to set European Monetary Union back on course. To be successful, they must find a way to achieve monetary union without creating the interest-rate disparities that have occurred in the past. If interest rates and monetary policies aren't in sync with one another, in whatever plan they come up with, any attempt to again tighten the trading band limits would be deemed premature by financial markets, leading to yet another wave of speculative attacks. A possible solution might be to group those nations with the strongest economies, allowing them to form a "mini-monetary union," while allowing struggling members to nurture their ailing economies. The outside nations, as they became able, could then join the monetary union later. This idea has been termed "two-speed Europe," and is not highly regarded by those wishing to see the EC advance collectively.

Conclusion

As we have seen, despite the obvious advantages of achieving a European Monetary Union, controversy and setbacks surround the idea. Issues are debated daily, and the effort sometimes seems like a continual uphill battle. Yet this struggle should be expected. The EC is comprised of nations with vastly different economies and cultures. Forcing them to converge too quickly would be akin to forcing a child to grow up prematurely—with similar unfortunate results. Dramatic changes, such as those that will be brought about by EMU, require a gestation period. They cannot be expected to happen overnight. There is little argument that EMU will occur eventually. The debate is over when it will occur and how it will be best achieved. For now, the plan in the Treaty of Maastricht is serving as the beacon toward a future enlightened Community with one currency and harmonious economic policies. There can be little doubt, however, that the beacon will be reflected many times, changing its form and evolving before finally illuminating Europe's monetary woes.

7

The Member Nations of the European Community

Territory is but the body of a nation. The people who inhabit its hills and valleys are its soul, its spirit, its life.

—James A. Garfield

An old English proverb states, "It takes all sorts to make a world." So too, does it take many nations to form a "European Community." The diversity of the EC's member nations is one of its most important assets. Domiciled within the Community's citizens are many cultures, languages and histories. It is not the intention of the Community, nor should it ever be, to coerce its citizens into diminishing the value of their various cultures. To guide Europe toward a colorless uniformity would be an atrocity ending in great loss. The EC's activities must be carefully directed so that they not only achieve desired political goals, but also respect the individuality of Europeans. The Community is, after all, the home of 342,000 million people first and a political entity second.

This chapter presents aspects of each of the Community's present member nations. It is hoped that this will provide a flavor of the individual countries, and an impression of how diverse the Community really is. Features of each member nation's culture, history and present state of affairs are presented. The chapter will be of some use when traveling within the EC, particularly for those visiting Europe for the first time. Some basic information on business practices in each member state has been included. So that certain *faux pas* are not committed at the expense of this book, as well as for curiosity's sake, a section is included for each nation detailing the more important characteristics of etiquette and protocol that are commonly observed in each land.

***

First, a few generalities. A passport is, of course, required when traveling anywhere within Europe. With the single market now completed, however, it is possible that an American arriving in the EC may be able to travel within the twelve countries and never need to present identification after the initial screening at the point of entry. Random checks at borders are, however, still possible, and the UK still insists on monitoring the inflow of persons into its territory.

As a general rule, US citizens may stay in EC countries for up to 90 days without any type of a visa or residence permit. Stays of more than 90 days require some form of temporary residence permit from the local authorities, which can be obtained by contacting any of the country's embassies worldwide. Citizens of the United States (or other foreigners) who wish to work in the Community are required to obtain a work permit. This also may be applied for at consulate offices and embassies, but generally one's employer takes care of these arrangements.

Every member of the EC is also a member of the United Nations and, of course, all are democracies. But beyond these broad similarities, the nations of the EC are a diverse group. Portugal, for example, is simply trying to build adequate roads and infrastructure while Germany is emerging as a world economic leader. Yet, each member state is, in one way or another, an asset to the Community, and all have aspirations for a bright future in a united Europe. The exploration of the member states will begin with Belgium, the center of many Community activities.

Belgium

Official Name:	Royaume de Belgique or
	Koninkrijk België (Kingdom of Belgium)
Population:	9.9 million
Population Density:	840 persons / mile^2 (325 /km^2)
Language(s):	Dutch (official), 57% and
	French (also official), 42%
Currency Unit:	Belgian Franc (recently 33.4 BF = $1)
Area:	11,783 miles^2, (30,516 km^2)
	—slightly larger than Maryland
Form of Government:	Constitutional Monarchy
Capital:	Brussels (Bruxelles)

Although Belgium is a small country—the distance between its two farthest points is only 175 miles (280 km)—it is generous in terms of appeal and history. The country's name is derived from a Celtic tribe, the Belgae, whom Julius Caesar referred to as being the most courageous tribe in all of Gaul. Respect for their courage, however, did not stop Caesar from invading their territory, and around 50 BC the area became a Roman province—a condition that would last for about 300 years. Belgium's strategic ports and fertile lands have caused it the woe of being a perpetual battleground for larger powers throughout history. Centuries of battles and campaigns to control the region have resulted in Belgium's present culture containing elements of Celtic, Roman, German, French, Dutch, Spanish and Austrian origin. In 1830 Belgium gained autonomy from the Netherlands through an uprising, and since then has largely maintained a policy of neutrality concerning external conflicts. In spite of its policy of neutrality, however, Belgium endured difficult occupations by Germany during both World Wars.

Belgium is one of the European Community's most enthusiastic supporters and it hopes to make its capital, Brussels, also the de facto capital of Europe. Brussels is effectively, though not yet officially, the headquarters of most EC institutions, including the Council and the Commission. The majority of Western Europe's capital cities are within 1000 km (625 miles) of Brussels, making it an ideal choice. Belgium is the second most densely populated country in the EC preceded only by the Netherlands, though its population is slowly declining. Nearly 95% of all Belgians live in cities.

Belgium is inhabited primarily by two broad groups of people—the Flemings (55%) and the Walloons (45%). The Flemings speak Flemish, a dialect of Dutch, and live mostly in the north-west portion of the country, which is called Flanders. Brussels is located in Flanders, yet ironically most of its inhabitants speak French. Nevertheless, the fact that bustling Brussels is in Flemish territory serves to reinforce the fact that the Flemish area of Belgium is heavily dedicated to, and dependent upon, commerce and industry. The Walloons speak French and inhabit the southeast part of Belgium—an area called Wallonie. Wallonie is mostly agricultural. Historically, the French language has dominated Flemish and was Belgium's only official language for centuries. It is only in modern times that Flemish has become a second official language of Belgium and some contention still exists regarding language. The Flemings cling zealously to their language, and Belgium is known for having an acute rivalry between speakers of its two national languages. It is, therefore, diplomatic to approach someone in Flanders using English or German rather than French.

Government

Belgium's government is a constitutional monarchy. The country's sovereign for the past 42 years, His Majesty Baudouin I, King of the Belgians, died in August 1993 of heart failure. His death was met with great sorrow by most Belgians because the king was a primary source of unity in a country that is otherwise dominated by political conflict between the Flemish and Walloons. King Baudouin was succeeded by his brother Prince Albert.

In the Belgian government, as in most other constitutional monarchies, the King appoints a prime minister and members of the cabinet. The Parliament consists of an upper and lower house. The lower house is known as the Chamber of Deputies, and consists of 212 members who are directly elected. The upper house, the Senate, has 182 members of which 106 are directly elected, 50 are chosen by provincial councils and 25 are co-opted. The one remaining member of the Senate is the heir to the throne. The primary political parties are the Flemish Christelijke Volkspartei (CVP) and its French speaking equivalent, the Parti social chrétien. Additionally, there are two liberal parties, the Flemish PVV and the French speaking PRL, as well as the Flemish and Walloon regional parties. There are three regional councils: Flanders, Wallonia and Brussels, and each is composed of the deputies and elected senators from each region.

Economy

Belgium's economy is centered around small private enterprises, though many large international corporations have moved there in recent years. It is a highly industrialized nation, with most of its industry concentrated in the north. Engineering, textile, paper, metal working, food processing and footwear companies make up the majority of Belgian industry. Belgians are specialists at converting imported raw materials into semi-finished goods and then exporting them.

American and Japanese firms are setting up offices in Brussels to take advantage of the single European market, while consultants and lawyers, both domestic and foreign, are reaping the benefits of helping digest the reams of new laws enacted by the EC.

Belgium has historically traded heavily with other nations. Lacking natural resources of its own, the country depends on imports for many essentials, and similarly must export many of its goods. Today, sixty percent of items produced in Belgium are exported, most of them to other EC nations.

Customs, Protocols, Etiquette & Some Suggestions

The Belgian people are tolerant toward foreigners and are very gracious hosts when entertaining. They are especially proud of their homes and a complement regarding one's home will always be well received. Initial contact with a member of the opposite sex should be confined to a handshake. Cheek kissing occurs only at a higher level of familiarity.

The key subject to avoid when speaking to a Belgian is the language division in the country. It is a very delicate topic. In business, formality is essential. Good dress and punctuality are expected. Belgians, in general, seek to be more efficient, reliable and quality conscious than their competitors, and expect their business associates to be the same.

Denmark

Official Name:	**Kongeriget Danmark (Kingdom of Denmark)**
Population:	**5.1 million**
Population Density:	**307 persons / mile^2 (119 /km^2)**
Language:	**Danish (official)**
Currency Unit:	**Danish Kroner (recently 6.2 Kroner = $1)**
Area:	**16,633 miles^2, (43,076 km^2)**
	—about twice the size of Massachusetts
Form of Government:	**Constitutional Monarchy**
Capital:	**Copenhagen (København)**

Denmark's history is full of valor, conquest and bravery. There was a time when the very mention of the word "Dane" would strike a vein of terror within hearts all across Europe. The Danish Empire once extended throughout the northern sea consisting of Norway, Sweden, Iceland and parts of Germany. The era of Viking conquest is long since over now, and the Danish people live today in what may be called one of the world's best functioning welfare states. This welfare system draws its origins from the socialist movements of the late 19th century which, owing to Denmark's strategic position at the northern tip of Europe, had reached Denmark via the same path that had earlier brought Christianity and then the Protestant Reformation. Prosperity seems to abound in Denmark today and life is comfortable and very organized. The welfare system, which has made evictions unheard of and supplied free housing to the elderly, recently gave the Danes one of the highest per-capita income tax rates in the EC, as well as a staggering high debt-per-capita of $7,000 per Dane. This provided Denmark with the contradictory honors of having both one of the highest standards of living in the world, and an enormous amount of debt-per-capita. Change was required both for harmonization with the EC and simply as a matter of insuring future prosperity. Presently, the Danish economy is among the healthiest in Europe.

Denmark joined the EC in 1973 and is the only Scandinavian member of the Community. The Danish see themselves as northern trailblazers, leading the way to the potential EC memberships of Norway, Sweden and Finland. In 1986, an important referendum showed that 56% of Danes supported the single-market concept. This outcome was significant because the influential Social Democratic Party was against the notion. It wanted Denmark to maintain its Scandinavian identity and was concerned that the single-market program would adversely affect relationships with the other Scandinavian countries. These fears were calmed, however, following a much-needed improvement in the Danish economy after a gloomy 1989-1990. Today, support for the EC is widespread and the single market has made many Danish businessmen confident in their country's otherwise uncertain future.

Danes generally react with stubborn resistance to outside pressure. This can be evidenced through the Danish rejection of the Treaty of Maastricht, which many Danes felt was forced upon them without adequate explanation. In a second referendum, the treaty was accepted by 57%, but this came only after a public-awareness program and some EC-granted concessions. The principal concessions allow the Dane's to later opt out of the treaty's plans for a common currency, common central bank and common defense.

Denmark is a small nation with a total land area of only about double that of the state of Massachusetts. It is an open-minded, tolerant nation with a deep sense of social welfare, a low crime rate and strong international connections. Danish, the official language, is used predominantly, but many Danes, particularly the younger generation, also speak English, German or both. The population of Denmark is 5.1 million with about 1.5 million Danish citizens living in the capitol city of Copenhagen. Most Danes are city dwellers—only 30% live in Denmark's rural areas. Denmark's population density of 119 persons per square kilometer puts it below the EC average of 144 persons per square kilometer. For comparison, the United States has an average 26 persons per square kilometer, or the state of New York has 131 persons per square kilometer.

Denmark is part of the Europe wide trend of decreasing population with birthrates falling from 2.37 children per woman in 1968 to 1.42 in 1988.

Government

The Danish Government is a constitutional monarchy, the sovereign presently being Queen Margrethe II. There is a 179-member Parliament called the Folketing, which has members elected by the citizens of Denmark for four year terms. Two Members of Parliament are elected from each of Denmark's two autonomous dependents: Greenland and the Faeroe Islands. The sovereign appoints a prime minister, who commands a majority in the Folketing. The prime minister, in turn, appoints a Cabinet or State Council, which is responsible to the Folketing.

The Danish Economy

Small firms dominate the Danish economy, with more than half the industrial work force being employed by firms with less than 200 people. Products produced in Denmark include clothing, textiles, foodstuffs, iron and steel products, chemicals, pharmaceuticals, machinery, beverages and leather. Its main agricultural products are wheat, barely, oats, rye, potatoes, sugar beets and tobacco. Having essentially no large industries to protect, Denmark is among the least protectionist of all European countries and has adopted easily to the common-market concept.

Foreign trade is very important to Denmark—about two-thirds of its gross domestic product comes from trade abroad. Fifty percent of Danish trade is with other EC member states. Many companies from other Nordic countries have established themselves in Denmark to gain access to the EC, and some US companies, such as Motorola, have also bought into Danish firms.

Its system of generous social benefits has caused Denmark to traditionally have some of the highest taxes in Europe. The standard value-added tax rate is presently 25%, but this is after attempts to bring it closer to the EC norm. Past decades have seen substantially higher rates.

Customs, Protocols, Etiquette & Some Suggestions

Danes have a sense of humor and are generally more interested in enjoying life than in power or politics. It must be noted, however, that most Danes have an obsession for punctuality. If you wish to impress a potential Danish client, do not be late.

To avoid being looked upon poorly by the Danes, be sure to know the difference between the various Scandinavian countries. A foreigner who can differentiate Denmark from Sweden, Norway and Finland—even to the slightest degree—will be more warmly accepted than one who lumps them all together.

Finally, don't choose the German occupation of Denmark during World War II as a casual conversation topic. In fact, to avoid inadvertently offending someone, World War II should always be treated delicately when dealing with any European.

France

UNITED KINGDOM

BELGIUM

GERMANY

LUX

English Channel

Lille
Pas-de-Calais
Arras• Nord
Somme
•Amiens Charleville-Mezieres
Seine- Laon
Maritime Oise Aisne Ardennes
Rouen •Beauvais Meuse •Metz
Moselle
Chalons-sur-Marne Bar-le-Duc •Nancy Strasbourg
Meurthe-et-Moselle Rhin
(Bas)

Channel Islands (U.K.)
Manche •Caen Eure Pontoise Val-d'Oise
Saint-Lô Calvados Evreaux• Yvelines ★Paris
Versailles• Seine- Marne
Orne Alencon Chartres Evry et-Marne
Essonne •Melun Aube
Eure-et-Loir •Troyes Chaumont Vosges •Epinal •Colmar
Marne Rhin
(Haute) (Haut)
•Vesoul Belfort
Saone
(Haute) •Besancon

Finistere St-Brieuc•
Cotes-du-Norde •Rennes Mayenne• Le Mans
•Quimper Ile-et-Vilaine •Laval Loiret
Morbihan Loire- Sarthe Blois •Orleans Auxerre
•Vannes Atlantique •Angers Tours Loir- Yonne Cote-d'Or
Maine- et-Cher Dijon
Nantes• et-Loire Indre-et-Loire Nievre Doubs
•Bourges Saone-et-Loire Jura SWITZERLAND
Chateauroux Cher Nevers Lons-le-Saunier
La Roche-sur-Yon Sevres •Poitiers Indre Moulins• Macon
Vendee (Deux) Vienne Allier •Bourg-en-Bresse
•Niort Ain Savoie (Haute)
•La Rochelle Gueret Rhone Annecy
Charente- Limoges• Creuse Clermont-Ferrand Lyon•
Maritime Angouleme Vienne (Haute) Puy-de-Dome St-Etienne Isere •Chambery
Charente Correze Loire Savoie
Nanterre Perigueux Tulle Cantal Le Puy Grenoble
•Bobigny Dordogne Aurillac Loire (Haute) •Valence Alpes ITALY
Paris (Haute)
•Creteil Lot Privas• Drome •Gap
Bordeaux Ardeche
Ile-de-France Gironde Lot-et- Cahors •Mende Digne Alpes-
Garonne Rodez Lozere Vaucluse Alpes de Maritimes
Agen• Tarn-et- Aveyron Gard •Avignon Haute-Provence Nice• MONACO
Landes Garonne •Albi Nimes Bouches-du-Rhône Var
Bay of Biscay Mont-de-Marsan Montauban Tarn Montpellier •Marseille
Gers •Auch Toulouse Herault •Toulon
Garonne
Pau• Tarbes (Haute) Carcassonne
Pyrenees- Pyrenees Foix Aude Gulf of Lions
Atlantique (Hautes) Ariege •Perpignan
ANDORRA Pyrenees-
Orientales

Bastia
Haute-
Corse

★ National Capital
Nice • City
——— International Boundary
——— Provincial Boundary
Lozere Province Name

0 Kilometers 200

SPAIN

Ajaccio•
Corse-
du-Sud

Official Name:	La République Française
	(The French Republic)
Population:	56 million
Population Density:	265 persons / mile^2 (102 /km^2)
Language:	French (official)
Currency Unit:	French Franc (recently 5.5 FF = $1)
Area:	211,208 miles^2, (546,986 km^2)
	—a little more than twice the size of Colorado
Form of Government:	Republic
Capital:	Paris

France has always held a special place in the hearts of story-tellers and dreamers, and, for many reasons, this praise is warranted. From the boulevards to the bistros, from Paris to Provence, the people of France approach life with a particular zeal that is distinctly "French." Distinctive tastes and a flair for the aesthetic are the general traits that are often accurately assigned to the French. The first French were the Gauls, a Celtic people, who were ultimately overcome by the legions of Julius Caesar and the Roman Empire, under which France became one of the most civilized areas in Europe. When the dominance of the Romans exhausted, a period of feudalism, marked by dissension and conflict, ensued until Charlemagne's Empire again brought order to the region. Later, in the 15th and 16th centuries, the Renaissance nurtured France into greatness, but the opulence of its royalty and upper class, as exemplified by the palace at Versailles and the dozens of others dotting the landscape, could be endured only so long by its impoverished lower class. On July 14, 1789, the Bastille (the state prison in Paris) was assailed by an angry Parisian mob, and the French Revolution was kicked off, destroying the monarchy and establishing a republic by 1790.

The next century witnessed the rise and fall of Napoleon, the Franco-Prussian war and the creation of a third French republic which lasted until World War I. World War II saw France occupied by Germany, and post World War II French history has been· a succession of sometimes conflicting policies desiring to restore France to world-class greatness and to integrate France with Europe.

French politicians have played a vital role in the promotion of the European Community and its ideas. France, along with its former bitter rival through three terrible wars, Germany, was one of the original founders of the European Community and a signatory of the Treaty of Paris.

Government

The French Republic has a somewhat unique governmental structure. Executive power is embodied in a president, elected by the French people for a seven year term. The president appoints a prime minister and a council of ministers, both of whom are responsible to Parliament, but it is the president who presides over the French Council of Ministers rather than the prime minister. Parliament is composed of two chambers. The upper house, the Senate, has 321 members, 13 of whom represent overseas departments and territories. All Senate members are elected by members of municipal, local and regional councils, except for 12 who are elected by French citizens resident abroad. Senators serve nine-year terms, with one-third of the Senate finishing their term every three years. The lower house is called the National Assembly, and comprises 577 deputies, including 22 for territories abroad. The members of the Assembly are elected for five-year terms.

The main political parties include the Socialist Party (PS), the conservative RPR, the centrist UDF (Union for French Democracy), the Communist PC, and the right-wing National Front (NF). In 1982, the 96 metropolitan political divisions, known as *départements,* were collected into 22 regions, which served to give local governments additional power.

The Economy

France is the second largest economy in the EC, preceded only by Germany, and the fourth largest in the world, with the US and Japan taking the number one and two positions. The industrial sector employs about one third of France's workers and contributes an equal percentage to the country's gross national product (GNP). During the period from 1982-1986 economic growth was sluggish. This trend reversed itself by late 1987 with strong consumer demand and later a surge in investment. This momentum has carried the economy along sufficiently; France began 1992 with a growth rate among the best in the EC.

France has a highly developed economy that operates on a large scale in areas as diverse as heavy industry, fashion, luxury goods and agriculture. The past decade has witnessed an ever increasing dependence on modern methods of production and this trend will no doubt continue as the country struggles to become a world class supplier of products from airplanes to vaccines. The agricultural sector has traditionally received large government subsidies, which have helped to make it the leading agricultural producer in Western Europe. These subsidies, however, are becoming the subject of increasing controversy in both world-trade talks and from the EC commission. As a result, they may decline in future years.

The list of weak points in the French economy is led by the nation's unemployment woes. The economy has had difficulty generating enough jobs for new entrants into the workplace. Unemployment averaged 9% from 1980 through 1992 and is estimated to be 11.5% in 1993. Besides the shear number of unemployed persons, the duration of joblessness has also become worse in the past two decades. In 1975, only 16.5% of those who were without work remained so for more than a year. This figure increased to 45.5% in 1987, and has since been reduced only slightly. France seems to have a long-term structural unemployment problem, and the officials of the French government are among many who sincerely hope the Single Market will promote growth, and thereby create more jobs. France is steadily advancing economic integration with the rest of the EC, and is one of just three member states who presently meet the stiff entry standards for European monetary union.

Customs, Protocols, Etiquette & Some Suggestions

When in France, always attempt to speak at least a little French. At a very minimum, know that *s'il vous plaît* (see voo play) means please, and *merci* (mehr si) means thank you. You will be better received if you attempt to communicate in French and fail, than if you don't try at all. In the end, it is likely that the French person you are talking to will speak at least some English, but you may be ignored if you *expect* him to adapt to you while you are in his country. In the business world, you are at a distinct disadvantage if you do not speak French. To complement the French, mention your respect for France and its culture and state your appreciation of French wine and cuisine (which is particularly excellent). Politics are a favorite topic of conversation and often lead to heated debates. Strikes by protesting employees, both public and private, are common and almost seem like an established part of French life—almost like a game.

Within the old French establishment, the atmosphere is still quite formal. Strict attention is paid to hierarchy and the use of titles such as *Monsieur le President* are always used when addressing the head of a firm or organization. Much of the younger generation has begun to deviate from the old ways, finding them a bit too repressing. Top heavy bureaucracies are being replaced, in many modern offices, by decentralized organizations which favor the use of first names over formal titles. Greetings of hello or good-bye should always be accompanied by a firm hand shake. A kiss on the cheek (never on the lips) will not shock a good friend of the opposite sex. When entering a room, greet everyone in the room and avoid the use of first names in formal situations. Other bits of general advice include never discussing the price of anything and not asking direct personal questions. The French appreciate unhurried, thorough discussions with plenty of facts— hasty decisions are rare. Finally, when speaking French in business situations, the informal form of you, *(tu),* should never be used. Always use the more formal *vous,* except when addressing children 15 years old or younger.

Germany

Legend:
- ⭐ National Capital
- Bonn • City
- International Boundary
- Administrative District Boundary
- *Bayern* Administrative District Name

0 — Miles — 100

DENMARK

Baltic Sea

North Sea

POLAND

NETHERLANDS

BELGIUM

LUX.

FRANCE

SWITZERLAND

CZECHOSLOVAKIA

AUSTRIA

Kiel •
Schleswig-
Holstein

• Rostock

Mecklenburg
• Schwerin

• Emden

• Bremerhaven • Hamburg

Bremen

Niedersachsen

⭐ Berlin

• Hanover

Magdeburg   Potsdam • *Brandenburg*

Saxony-Anhalt

Halle •

Nordrhein-Westfalen

• Leipzig

• Dusseldorf

Dresden •

Koln •

Erfurt •   Chemnitz •
Thuringia

Bonn •

Hessen   • Suhl

Frankfurt •
• Wiesbaden
Mainz

Rhineland-Pfalz

Saarland
Saarbrucken

• Nurnberg

• Regensburg

Bayern

• Stuttgart

• Augsburg
• Munich

Baden-Wurttemberg

• Freiburg

Official Name:	Bundesrepublik Deutschland
	(The Federal Republic of Germany)
Population	
(unified):	78.6 million
(West):	62.0 million
(East):	16.6 million
Population Density	
(unified):	570 persons / mile^2 (220 /km^2)
(West):	646 persons / mile^2 (249 /km^2)
(East):	397 persons / mile^2 (153 /km^2)
Language:	German (official)
Currency Unit:	Deutsche Mark (recently 1.6 DM = $1)
Area	
(unified):	137,860. miles^2 (357,029. km^2)
	—88% the size of California
(West)	96,032. miles^2 (248,704. km^2)
(East)	41,828. miles^2 (108,325. km^2)
Form of Government:	Federal Republic
Capital:	Berlin

Germany is the EC's economic locomotive. It is the third most powerful economy in the world, behind the USA and Japan. It leads the other member states in terms of trade surplus, gross national product, and world trade, and has been able to maintain desirably low levels of inflation and unemployment while other EC countries struggled with these problems. To a large degree, the success of the German economy can be credited to the strict discipline of its central bank, the Bundesbank. The Bundesbank has steadfastly avoided temptations to change policies for short-term gains, favoring, instead, decisions based on long-term wisdom. In October 1990, Germany tackled the immense project of reunification with its Eastern half, which was finally released from the Communist grasp that has embraced it since shortly after World War II.

The collapse of the Berlin Wall, perhaps the most symbolic act of the demise of Communism, began in the late 1980s. Sweeping reforms by Gorbachev in the Soviet Union prompted widespread demands for greater freedom in East Germany. But the policies of the aging East German communist government, led by Eric Hoenecker, were unresponsive to these demands. By 1989, discontent grew to such a level that untold masses of East German citizens began fleeing their captor nation via Poland, Czechoslovakia and Hungary. Massive pro-reform demonstrations occurred in East German cities, leading to the assignment of a new leader, Egon Krenz. The Wall was subsequently taken down in November 1990, allowing free movement between the east and west halves of Berlin for the first time since 1961. Demonstrations continued urging further change in East Germany, and Egon Krenz was replaced by a non-Communist government, including a president and a prime minister.

Free elections were held in East Germany, for the first time since World War II, in March 1990, and West German Chancellor Helmut Kohl saw his center-right Christian Democrat party receive a substantial share of the East German people's votes—the Communist party was reduced to a minority. Chancellor Kohl put forth the idea of monetary union between the two Germanys and East German Ostmarks became valuable West German Deutsche marks overnight on July 2, 1990. This move made the campaign for German reunification virtually unstoppable. In February 1990, negotiations between the two Germanys and the USA, France, Britain and the USSR, the wartime allies who had originally divided Germany, began. Initial resistance from the USSR was overcome, and Germany was granted permission to reunite and to maintain membership in NATO and the EC in its reunited form. Officially, German reunification occurred on October 3, 1990, and the first all Germany elections were held in December 1990.

The reunification has proven to be even more taxing on the German economy than anticipated, yet the former West German government is, as they must be, wholly dedicated to ensuring its success at whatever cost. It is not an easy undertaking. The 17 million citizens of former East Germany have habits ingrained by 40 years of communist rule and are used to the guarantees, however stark they may be, of a centralized government. Instilling habits of initiative and an entrepreneurial spirit are daunting tasks because the region has not known freedom since the 1933 arrival of the Nazis.

Despite the difficulties met during reunification, Germany is still healthy economically and its Bundesbank sets the pace for all the other central banks of Europe, particularly those participating in the Exchange Rate Mechanism (see chapter 6). Since its reunification, Germany is poised to once again become Europe's largest and wealthiest nation—a situation which has meant disaster historically. This time, however, Germany has devoted itself to the policies of a united Europe, endorsed by the European Community it helped found. The perceived threat of Germany as an economic competitor, and not a military aggressor, by other European nations is testimony to the success of the Community's aspirations.

Germany has a vested interest in helping East European countries build their own solid market economies because, at present, Germany is the destination of choice for disgruntled Romanian or Czechoslovakian workers. Under law enacted after World War II, Germany must accept ethnic Germans who resettled in Eastern Europe and the former Soviet Union during the war. Thus far, over a million have come back and there is potential for as many as 10 million more if things do not improve economically in the East.

Government

The government of Germany is a Federal Republic similar to that of the United States, which helped form it after the Second World War. With the incorporation of former East Germany, Germany is now composed of 16 Länder (states). Each Länd is represented in the 68-member upper house of Parliament, the Bundesrat (Federal Council), by either three, four or six representatives depending on its population. These members are appointed for a limited time. The lower house is called the Bundestag (Federal Assembly), and has 652 members which are elected by the populace under a mixed system of proportional representation and fixed single-member constituencies for four year terms. A federal chancellor (currently Helmut Kohl) is elected by the Bundestag. The chancellor heads the federal government which is responsible for performing the nation's executive duties. A federal president is elected for a five-year term by vote from a combined assembly of the Bundesrat and an equal number of representatives of each of the Länder. Each Länd has its own Government and Parliament. The primary political parties include the conservative Christian Democratic Union (CDU), the socialist Social Democratic Party (SPD), its Bavarian equivalent the Christian Social Union, the liberal Free Democratic Party (FDP), the green party (Die Grünen) and the former East German Communist party, the Party of Democratic Socialism (PDS).

The official federal capital of Germany was moved from Bonn back to Berlin in October 1990, and a transition period is currently in progress. The upper house of the German Parliament, the Bundesrat, will remain in Bonn, but will be among little company as the chancellor's office, the chief ministries, and the main house of Parliament, the Bundestag, have all begun moving to Berlin. The embassies which have accumulated in and around Bonn over the last 43 years will also be uprooted and moved east to the new capital of 4.3 million.

The Economy

Due to its lack of natural resources (coal being the exception), Germany's economy is dominated by manufacturing and service-oriented businesses. Automobiles, heavy machinery, banking, finance, and insurance are among the most prominent examples of the types of goods and services that have led this industrial nation out of ruin since World War II.

By far the most important influence on the German economy in recent years, if not decades, is the highly acclaimed reunification of East and West Germany. The years since the unification have consisted intermittently of euphoria and pessimism. One constant, however, is that the West has poured money into the East in hopes of balancing the nation. The western half of the economy saw a boom in 1989 and 1990 spurred by huge demand for western goods in the east. Meanwhile, the eastern economy collapsed as the obsolete nature of its structure became painfully evident. Hundreds of billions of German marks have been spent on efforts to invigorate the ailing eastern economy, but the results are slow. Currently, one out of every four former East Germans are still looking for permanent positions. Eventually, however, economists expect eastern Germany will be a net contributor to the growth of united Germany as it carries its role as a major economic power into the coming decades.

Customs, Protocols, Etiquette & Some Suggestions

The fact that Teutonic discipline is legendary is testimony to the German people's dedication toward quality, organization and thoroughness. Germans have a well-earned reputation for being extremely efficient and serious in matters concerning politics and business. Successful interaction with them in these areas will require replicating their qualities. Be punctual for appointments, and attempt to plan out agendas well in advance so that meetings are never impromptu by necessity. Business meetings should not be suggested to take place over breakfast, as this is not a common practice, and avoid using first names in formal atmospheres unless your German counterpart does first.

Greece

Official Name:	Ellenikí Dimokrátia (Hellenic Republic) or Ellás (Greece)
Population:	10 million
Population Density:	196 persons / mile^2 (76 / km^2)
Language:	Greek (official)
Currency Unit:	Greek Drachma (recently 220 drachma = $1)
Area:	50,944 miles^2, (131,937 km^2) —slightly smaller than Alabama
Form of Government:	Republic
Capital:	Athens (Athînai)

Greece is a land rich in mythology and history dating back millenniums. It is a country of contrasts and finds itself struggling between past glory and present difficulties. Today's struggles center on trying to modernize its economy while preserving its culture. It seems to be slowly succeeding.

The European Community has invested an undisclosed 10 to 20 billion ECUs in Greece in an attempt to bring its economy and standard of living up to the EC average. History has seen Greece as the beneficiary of European aid before, as Greece owes its independence to the 1827 naval Battle of Navarino where the navies of Britain, France and Russia decidedly defeated a joint Turkish-Egyptian fleet. This rescue enduringly freed Greece from the Ottoman Empire for the first time in centuries. Subsequent rule by European Monarchs, such as Otto I of Bavaria and later King George I of Denmark, were uneventful and ended when King George I was ousted in 1909. The period since then has been marked by turmoil. A republican government was subsequently put in place, but was short lived. In 1935, a monarchy was restored, but it was not to survive the influences of the two World Wars. A coalition of conservative parties eventually emerged after World War II, but was overcome by a military coup in 1967. The military dictators were expelled in 1974, due to the fear that all out war with Turkey would result from their policies. Subsequently, a constitution was drawn up and the present 300-member parliament was formed. Greece joined the EC in 1981. A major financial scandal (the Koskotas affair) involving the chairman of the Bank of Crete, George Koskotas, embarrassed the nation in 1988, and combined with other events to bring down the then in power Panhellenic Socialist Party (PASOK)—this was followed by a string of temporary governments and general political instability. Finally, in 1990, the present leadership, the conservative New Democracy Party (NDP), came into power by a narrow margin after winning the third of three general elections held in the space of only 10 months. The new government, under the leadership of Prime Minister Constantine Mitsotakis, has been able to reestablish international credibility and has expressed dedication toward taking the actions necessary to enable Greece to be a full partner in the European Community and take full advantage of the Single Market. This dedication is, in a sense, mandatory, because the EC is growing impatient with Greece's slow advancement. It has placed Greek policies under its surveillance, pledging that all future EC grants will be combined with more severe supervision to see that they are properly used. In a sense, Greece's association with the EC has condemned it to succeed.

Government

The government of Greece currently consists of a 300-member Parliament which is elected by the Greek population under a system of proportional representation. The president is elected for a five-year term by the Parliament and is responsible for appointing a prime minister and other ministers. The prime minister commands a majority in the Parliament.

The Economy

Agriculture is vital to the Greek economy, as it employs over a quarter of the labor force and accounts for a fifth of the country's exports. Manufacturing accounts for only about 20% of the nation's gross national product. The other largest contributor is tourism.

Major Greek industries are motor vehicle assembly, textiles, food processing and cement. Greek farms produce barley and wheat, olives, corn, tobacco, cotton, citrus and other fruits. Fruits and vegetables are one of Greece's primary exports, the others include textiles, iron, steel, nickel, aluminum, petroleum products, ships and tobacco. Greece imports virtually all the raw materials it uses as well as almost all luxury goods and industrial products. Most industrial activity is concentrated in Athens, with some spilling out to other Greek cities such as Salonika, Patras,

Volos and Larissa. Greece's primary trading partners are Italy and Japan. France also trades significantly with the Greeks.

Greece must undertake major restructuring before it will be able to achieve its goal of becoming a full fledged member of the European Monetary System. The drachma has historically fallen 10% to 12% per year against the reference German mark—with the blessing of the Greek central bank. This devaluation has been used as a method to combat Greece's strong inflation, which was 20.4% in 1990. In 1992, inflation was slowed to around 15%, but Greece still had the worst rate in the Community.

Fundamental structural changes need to be accomplished to permanently tackle the inflation problem. The mentality of allowing the drachma to continually be devalued as a weapon against inflation is akin to using mending tape to repair a failing dam. Additionally, one of the requirements for entry into the EMS is that the subject country's currency not have been devalued for two years prior to adopting fixed exchange rates.

Customs, Protocols, Etiquette & Some Suggestions

The people of Greece are relaxed and casual in manner and don't generally take things too seriously if their immediate well being is not threatened. Greek hospitality is sincere and abundant and should be returned to forge lasting relationships with Greek nationals. The lifestyle in Greece is quite casual—epitomized by the eternal nighttime gatherings at taverns with tables full of food, wine and friends. Spontaneity and a relaxed carefree manner are characteristics for which Greeks are known, and occasionally these traits may result in a Greek business contact being late for a meeting. This casualness is met with hypocrisy, however, as the Greeks expect punctuality from others, particularly foreigners. Business meetings in Greece can be extremely long affairs, as Greeks expect to spend as much time as required to work out details. This should be taken into account when planning an agenda around a business meeting. Business people generally dress conservatively, and the apparel is lightweight during the hot months from mid-May through September. The weather is cooler and rainier during the winter months, so appropriately heavier clothes are the norm.

Many Greeks in Athens and the resort towns speak English. In particular, most young Greeks or people in business are likely to speak English—those living in rural areas will probably not. It is wise to familiarize yourself with the Greek alphabet, and carry a guide book with some basic translations. "Né," confoundedly, means "yes" and when Greeks silently closes their eyes or click their tongues while lifting their eyebrows, they are signaling "no." Body language can lead to many misunderstandings, so be sure you've understood what a gesture means before acting on it. Waving a hand up and down doesn't mean "good-bye," or "stay there," but implies "come." The gesture of tilting and bowing the head in one motion indicates "yes," or "affirmative."

Ireland

National Capital
Lifford • City
—— International Boundary
—— County Boundary
Donegal County Name

0   Miles   50

North Channel

Creeslough

Letterkenny •

Donegal   Lifford •   **NORTHERN IRELAND (U.K.)**

• Ardara

Donegal

Donegal Bay

Lower Lough Erne

Lough Neagh

Sligo *Leitrim*

Upper Lough Erne

Monaghan

Sligo

Monaghan

• Bangor Erris   Ballina •

Lough Conn

Lough Allen   • Cavan

Carrick on Shannon

Cavan

Dundalk •

Mayo   Charlestown •

• Castlebar

Roscommon

Longford

Lough Sheelin

Liouth

Drogheda

Irish Sea

• Westport

Claremorris •

Longford

Meath

Lough Mask

Roscommon •

Lough Ree

• Navan

• Mullingar

• Trim

• Tuam

Westmeath

Athlone

• Clifden

Lough Corrib

• Galway

Galway

Offaly

• Tullamore

Naas •

★ **Dublin**

Port Laoise

Kildare

Laois

Wicklow

Wicklow

North Atlantic Ocean

• Ennistimon

Ennis •

Lough Derg

Clare

• Roscrea

Nenagh •

Durrow •

Carlow •

Arklow •

• Kilkee

• Limerick

Tipperary

Carlow

Kilkenny

Kilkenny •

Limerick

• Tipperary

Caher •   • Clonmel

Wexford

Wexford •

Rosslare

• Tralee

Kerry

Mallow •   Fermoy •

Dungarvan •

Waterford

Waterford

Kilarney •

Cork

Youghal •

Kenmare

• Macroom   • Cork

Saint Georges Channel

• Bantry

Official Name:	**Poblacht na h'Éireann (Republic of Ireland)**
Population:	**3.5 million**
Population Density:	**129 persons / mile² (50 /km²)**
Language(s):	**Irish, i.e., Gaelic (official), English**
Currency Unit:	**Irish Punt (recently 1 punt = $1.5)**
Area:	**27,136 miles², (70,278 km²)**
	—slightly larger than West Virginia
Form of Government:	**Republic**
Capital:	**Dublin**

Throughout ancient times the mysterious island of Ireland represented the outermost boundary of man's knowledge of the world. Its remote north-west location places it such that its western extremities occupy the furthest west longitudes in Europe. Nicknamed the Emerald Isle, Ireland was seized by Henry II for England in the 12th Century—an action which has kept the island embroiled in conflict even to this day. The English occupation led to much land being taken from the native inhabitants and given to English settlers. This resulted in sharp class divisions wherein there existed a dominant, landowning class, and a dependent, landless class. Further conflicts where caused by the English being predominantly Protestants, and the Irish mostly Roman Catholics. This clashing state of affairs has caused continual fighting and wars throughout the centuries. In the 17th and 18th century, legislation was passed which discriminated against Roman Catholics and favored Protestants. The degree of discrimination varied from mild to blatant, but even the mildest cases added fuel to the flames burning in hearts of angered Roman Catholics. On Easter day in 1916 an unsuccessful rebellion against English dominance occurred when the Dublin Easter Rising took place. Despite its failure, disorder ensued and with the exception of the primarily Protestant northeast, the British administration in Ireland became dysfunctional. Most Irish police officers resigned and were replaced by British officers. Fighting broke out between Irish nationalists and British military and police—by 1919 Ireland was engulfed in violence. Five years of war followed from 1916 to 1921, resulting in the Island being divided into the Irish Free State and Northern Ireland—Northern Ireland being the north eastern corner of the island who wished to remain a part of the UK. The Irish Free State, proclaimed in 1922, was not accepted by those who wanted an Irish republic, which led to civil war. The civil war ultimately resulted in the Irish Free State becoming the Republic of Eire in 1937. The Republic of Eire remained neutral during World War II. Following the second World War, in 1949, an agreement was reached by which the Republic of Eire became the Republic of Ireland and was declared a sovereign, independent state. The Republic of Ireland joined the EC in 1973.

With a population of only 3.5 million, the entire country of Ireland has only half as many people as London or Paris, and represents only 1% of the population of the European Community. On average, the population of Ireland is young—about half the country's residents are under 25. These young people are generally well educated and provide one of Ireland's most important resources—its bright, young work force.

Government

The government of the Republic of Ireland is led by an elected president who serves a seven-year term. There is a parliament that consists of two houses, a house of representatives (Dail Eireann), consisting of 166 members and a 60-member senate (Seanad Eireann). The legal system is based on English common law, but has been substantially modified by local concepts.

The Economy

Although over 80% of Irish soil is used for farming, industry has surpassed agriculture as the most important economic sector on this island nation. The slight population of Ireland makes the Irish economy small and trade dependent, but it is open and competitive, and the Irish have been feverishly working to join the more advanced EC countries by the year 2000. All and all, these efforts seem to be slowly paying off.

The double digit inflation that burdened the nation in the late 1970s has been brought down to acceptable levels, and the reckless borrow-and-spend mentality of the government has been placed under control. But unemployment remains a serious problem. In 1992, over 16% of the Irish work force remained jobless, giving the Emerald Island the worst rate of unemployment in the Community. To combat unemployment, the Irish government has embarked on a campaign to attract foreign investment, and US companies have responded with the most enthusiasm. Many US corporations, spurred by a desire to win a piece of the Single European Market, have sought to establish a European presence, and many have chosen Ireland as the place to do it. Among those who have expanded into Ireland are AT&T, Apple, IBM, GE, NEC, Kodak and 14 major pharmaceutical companies. Many American software companies, such as Microsoft, have also been drawn to Ireland. The US is by far the biggest foreign investor in Ireland with 350 companies that employ about 40,000 people. To attract these companies, the Irish government has provided investment incentives such as a corporate tax rate of only 10% (Western Europe's lowest) that is guaranteed until the year 2000.

Customs, Protocols, Etiquette & Some Suggestions

The Irish are sociable people with a well developed sense of humor, though a few cautions can be appropriately recommended to foreigners who visit Ireland. The taboo topic of the division of North Ireland from the Republic of Ireland should never be ventured into by a non-Irish. Furthermore, though they drive on the same side of the road, dress similarly, enjoy their ales and speak the same tongue, the Irish should never be considered English. They are Irish, and they value their nationality highly. Though the Irish are accommodating and friendly people, they are liable to take offense easily, so mind your manners.

One last word, avoid the use of the word Eire, both in verbal and written communication. Although it is Gaelic for Ireland, it is only acceptable when speaking or writing in Gaelic. When communicating in English use Ireland. Letters should be addressed to the Republic of Ireland.

Italy

Official Name:	Italia (Italy) or
	Repubblica Italiana (Republic of Italy)
Population:	57 million
Population Density:	490 persons / mile^2 (189 /km^2)
Language:	Italian (official)
Currency Unit:	Lira (recently 1,472 lira = $1)
Area:	116,319 miles^2, (301,248 km^2)
	—slightly larger than Arizona
Form of Government:	Republic
Capital:	Rome (Roma)

Thoughts of Roman chariot races, Caesars, the Renaissance, Michelangelo, Da Vinci, Rome, Venice, the Vatican, fashion, design and extraordinary cuisine are all conjured up when thinking of Italy. Appropriately renowned for its art, culture and vibrant history, Italy has also become notable for its political disorder, bureaucratic inefficiencies, problems with corruption and gross public spending woes. Since the Fascist government of Mussolini, which was removed after the allied invasion of Sicily in 1943, the rise and fall of elected governments has been staggering. The present administration—operating, unfortunately, on equally uncertain ground—is the 51st since World War II. As a result of decades of excessive government spending, and some of the most generous social benefits in the world, Italy's public debt now exceeds its gross national product. Radical reforms are being introduced to attempt to alleviate the debt, but are being met with severe opposition by many, realizing that the sacrifices imposed by the reforms will be felt for many years.

In spite of these difficulties, the aspirations of Italian leaders to transform their country into one of the most economically healthy nations in the European Community remain high and unfettered. Italy's participation in the European Community and the Single Market is treated enthusiastically, as Italian entrepreneurs see the removal of trade barriers as a chance to broaden the area in which they can practice their well-earned reputation as being masterful salesmen.

Government

The government of Italy is somewhat chaotic by most western country's standards. To exemplify the extent of Italy's bureaucratic mess, consider that Italian companies hire full-time, well-educated, well-paid individuals simply to deal with the complexities and inefficiencies of the Italian bureaucracy. This often consists of simply knowing which line to wait in and which forms to fill out—a task that is frequently complex and discouraging. In a recent Italian court case, an individual was held liable for entrusting an important package to the Italian mail! Recent shake-ups, however, have finally seen genuine advances in the struggle to topple corruption in Italian industry and government, and they may pave the way to a more stable future.

The Italian government has a president, a prime minister and a two-house parliament consisting of the upper chamber or Senate, and a lower chamber or Chamber of Deputies. The Senate has 315 members who are elected by citizens of age 25 years or older to represent the regions. The chamber of deputies has 630 members who are elected by citizens aged 18 and over. The president is elected for a seven-year term, and appoints the prime minister. The main political parties are the conservative Christian Democrat Party, the Democratic Party of the Left, which was formerly the Communist party, the PSI socialist party, the RPI republican party, the Radical Party and the Liberal Party. Italy is divided into 20 regions, each of which has its own regional government.

The Economy

Italy is the world's fifth largest economy in terms of gross national product, yet it remains persistently divided economically between the north and south. Regional differences in income per person and unemployment rates are larger in Italy than in any other EC country. The purchasing power of citizens in the North exceeds the average of the more affluent European countries, yet in the South it is on a level with Spain and barely higher than Portugal or Greece. The advanced and prosperous north, with its wealth and contemporary methods, exists in sharp contrast to the poor and under industrialized south, whose primarily agrarian population is resistant to change.

Industry in the northern regions of Italy is well-developed, and manufactures such things as electrical and electronic goods, clothing, cars, leather goods and china. Since 1983, the Italian economy has enjoyed a slow but steady economic expansion, but 1991's growth of 1.4% was the smallest seen since 1983 and the current situation doesn't offer any easy methods of improvement. The 1990s present many challenges to Italy, including continuing to cleanse itself of corruption, refurbishing its laughable telecommunications system, controlling industrial pollution, and adjusting to its ongoing integration with the rest of the European Community.

Customs, Protocols, Etiquette & Some Suggestions

In Italy, being up to an hour late is being on time for an appointment. Punctuality is generally not part of the Italian demeanor. Ardent hand shaking and extroverted behavior, however, is. Italians communicate with their entire bodies, often waving their arms in attempts to make their point better understood. Indeed, Italians seem to have a particular zeal for life, and are generally uninhibited in demonstrating it. When dealing with Italians, it is you, not them, who must accommodate the other's different tempo and culture. In business, Italians are energetic negotiators who will often be impeccably dressed and flawlessly groomed—style pervades the Italian psyche.

Luxembourg

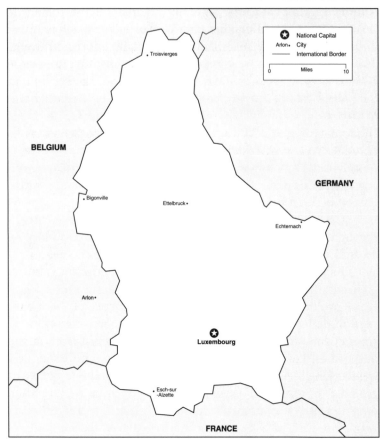

Official Name:	Grand-Duché de Luxembourg
	(Grand Duchy of Luxembourg)
Population:	377,000
Population Density:	378 persons / mile^2 (146 /km^2)
Languages:	French (official), Letzeburgish (national)
	and German
Currency Unit:	Luxembourg Franc
	(identical to Belgian Franc)
Area:	998 miles^2, (2,585 km^2)
	—slightly smaller than Rhode Island
Form of Government:	Constitutional Monarchy
Capital:	Luxembourg City

"Every Luxembourger is a famous Luxembourger because he is known by all the other Luxembourgers." This statement by George Erasmus in a commentary on Luxembourg sums up the undeniable fact that Luxembourg is a small country. With only 998 square miles in its domain, it is roughly 80% the size of Rhode Island. While it is the smallest member of the EC, it is also the richest on a per capita basis, and enjoys a very high standard of living.

Founded in 963 AD, Luxembourg is an aged country with a battle scarred past resulting from ceaseless raids and occupations by the French, Burgundians (of Burgundy), Spaniards, Austrians and Germans. These invasions most recently ended with a French occupation, but the last French soldier left Luxembourg in 1867, enabling the tiny country to establish its neutrality through the Treaty of London. Since that time, Luxembourg has created a reputation as being peace loving and independent.

This independence has been tested by opposition from foreign countries regarding Luxembourg's banking secrecy laws, which are the strictest in the world. The presence of these banking policies have made Luxembourg a favorite depository of money from clients worldwide. Despite periodic criticism from outside authorities, Luxembourg added additional strength to its existing banking secrecy laws in March 1989, making it virtually impossible for any investigating tax authority to penetrate a Luxembourg bank account. Luxembourg banks will, however, always cooperate with investigating authorities if they can provide sufficient evidence to show that the funds in question were derived from criminal activity. This cooperation was demonstrated, for example, in 1990 when investigating authorities were allowed to access the accounts of various drug barons and General Noriega, ex-dictator of Panama, and again in 1991 during the Bank of Credit and Commerce International (BCCI) scandal. It should be noted, however, that tax-evasion is *not* considered a criminal offense in Luxembourg and suspicion of tax-evasion is definitely not sufficient grounds for revealing the details of an account there.

Government

Luxembourg's government is a constitutional monarchy headed by a Grand Duke or Duchess as sovereign. There is a 60-person Chamber of Deputies whose members are elected for five years under a system of proportional representation through universal adult voting. The sovereign appoints a Council of Ministers and a President of the Council (Premier), who commands a majority of the Chamber. The primary political parties are the Social Christian Party (center-right), the Socialist Party and the Democratic Party (liberal).

The Economy

Luxembourg is associated with neighboring Belgium through the Belgium-Luxembourg Economic Union (BLEU), and shares Belgium's currency and customs facilities. Close integration is also maintained with the Netherlands. Its own recent history has taught the small country that over-reliance on one sector of the economy can be devastating should that industry collapse, as happened in the steel industry during the 1970s. That downturn left a large dent in the Luxembourg economy. Now, the iron and steel industry, which was originally based on local ore, is becoming considerably more diversified, as is the entire industrial sector of Luxembourg. Steel has benefited from a worldwide upturn and continues to represent a large percentage of Luxembourg's gross domestic product. Luxembourg has, however, also become a major international banking center. Presently, banking and other services have become the country's largest provider of revenue. Overall, Luxembourg has become one of the healthiest economies in Europe (if not the world). It consistently shows budget surpluses, positive trade balances and low inflation combined with low unemployment.

Customs, Protocols, Etiquette & Some Suggestions

Luxembourgers zealously guard their national identity, and should not be considered as vaguely French, German or Belgian. In general, Luxembourgers are friendly, and enjoy using their considerable language skills. Any attempt to use simple phrases in the national language, Letzeburgish, are appreciated. French is the most popular language in Luxembourg, though Letzeburgish and German are also official languages of the country. English is well understood in business circles, though it is better to use French for business dealings, if possible. The business environment is quite formal. Dress and mannerisms are conservative and hand shaking is common.

As in any country, Luxembourgers appreciate a foreigner who has some understanding of their country's history and culture. This may be particularly important in Luxembourg, though, because it demonstrates awareness of the tiny country's distinct, independent status. Luxembourg has boundaries with Belgium, France and Germany, so developments in these countries are important to the people of Luxembourg. But be careful not to speak only of outside developments. Topics of discussion relating to the development of Luxembourg, its language and culture are popular. Other general topics of conversation include automobiles, which Luxembourgers generally regard as highly prestigious, and family. If invited to a family house in Luxembourg, a bouquet of flowers for the lady of the house would be considered thoughtful.

Netherlands

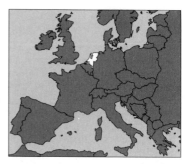

Official Name:	**Koninkrijk der Nederlanden**
	(The Kingdom of the Netherlands)
Population:	**14.7 million**
Population Density:	**916 persons / mile^2 (354 /km^2)**
Language(s):	**Dutch (official)**
Currency Unit:	**Guilder (recently 1.8 guilder = $1)**
Area:	**16,042 miles^2, (41,546 km^2)**
	—just less than twice the size of New Jersey
Form of Government:	**Constitutional Monarchy**
Capital:	**Amsterdam**
Seat of Government:	**The Hague (Den Haag)**

The Netherlands is the most densely populated country in the EC with over 900 people per square mile. One million of these people live in the capital city of Amsterdam, which is capital in name only—virtually all governmental offices are located in the Netherlands's seat of government, the Hague. The Hague is located 34 miles south-west of Amsterdam and is frequently the location of important international meetings and conferences. The official language of the Netherlands is Dutch, although English, German and French are also widely spoken and understood.

If childhood has left you with an image of the Netherlands consisting of windmills, tulips and golden fields stretching to the horizon, you wont be disappointed when you arrive there. Outside the country's few cities, the storybook image paints a rather realistic picture of what the Netherlands is like. The country is famous for its series of dikes and sea-walls that protect it from the encroachment of the sea, but the sea actually has rightful ownership of much of the land—one quarter of the Netherlands's territory is below sea-level.

During the 17th century, the Netherlands served as Europe's center of banking and arms manufacture and was involved in vast trading all over the world. The most infamous transaction of the Dutch is, perhaps, the purchase of what is today Manhattan Island from the Manhattan Indians for a mere pittance by the Dutch East and West Indies Company. Seventeenth century Netherlands had a renowned reputation of being a remarkably open intellectual forum. Due to this reputation, Holland has a long tradition of cultivating extraordinary minds, particularly within the arts. Many great painters, probably the most famous of which is

Rembrandt, came from the Netherlands, further glorifying its rich past. The glamour attained during the 17th century faded away gradually during the 18th century during a period of French occupation, but then entered a phase of rejuvenation under the monarchs of the 19th century.

The Netherlands was neutral during World War I, but endured occupation by Nazi Germany from 1940 to 1945. During the occupation, the Dutch resistance bravely assisted the Dutch Jews. Following the second World War, a fierce colonial war ensued in the Dutch East Indies, which had been under Dutch control since the 17th century. Under international pressure, the Dutch established that they could no longer maintain control of the colony and it became independent as Indonesia.

The politics of the past few decades have been traditionally very liberal, aspiring toward the formation of an egalitarian utopia. This aspiration has not materialized, however, and the Netherlands is beginning to change its manner of politics. The result of the policies of past decades has resulted in an ultra-expensive welfare state with 3.4 million unemployed workers who receive unemployment benefits that amount to more than the minimum wage. Only slightly more, 4.5 million, work to support them and the system. This state of affairs clearly must change, and current policies are aimed at streamlining the unemployment benefit system.

The Netherlands was one of the original six founding members of the EC and is very pro European Community. Fully 82% of the population, the highest in the Community, support the EC's integration efforts. Only 4% say they are against the EC.

Government

The Netherlands is a constitutional monarchy; the current sovereign is Her Majesty Queen Beatrix, who took the throne upon the abdication of her mother on April 30, 1980. The government's organization consists of two Chambers: the primary consists of 75 members and is called the First Chamber of the States-General, the secondary has 150 members and is called simply the Second Chamber. Members of the States-General are elected by the councilmen of the 12 provincial councils of the Netherlands and serve six-year terms, with half the members departing every three years. Members of the Second Chamber are elected by universal adult suffrage for a four-year term under a system of proportional representation. As in many other constitutional monarchies, the monarch is responsible for appointing a prime minister. The prime minister then commands a majority in the States-General and, in turn, appoints a Council of Ministers who are responsible to the States-General. There are many political parties in the Netherlands, the primary ones being the conservative Christian Democratic Appeal (CDA) Party, the PvdA Labor Party, the liberal VVD Peoples Party for Freedom and Democracy, and the D66, or Democracy 66 Party.

The Economy

The Dutch people have always been business oriented and the country is highly industrialized. The standard of living is quite high, despite having relatively few natural resources (except natural gas). The Netherlands is a leading exporting nation, and its prosperity, thereby, depends to a great deal on the prosperity of the nations that purchase its goods. Presently, Germany consumes almost 30 percent of the Dutch exports, and this figure stands to increase as the reunification with former East Germany matures and enhances its demand for goods. Primary exported products include natural gas, chemicals, agricultural and dairy produce, and machinery. The Netherlands is home to the world's largest port. The shipping port in Rotterdam handles some 290 million tons of freight per year from over 30,000 vessels, which makes the port in Kobe, Japan, at 175 million tons per year, only a distant second.

Primary industries in the Netherlands are agriculture, flowers, machinery, motor vehicles, shoes, textiles, electronics, foodstuffs, natural gas, tobacco products, building materials, and shipbuilding. The major imported products are crude oil, most raw materials, cars and trucks, and foodstuffs.

Customs, Protocols, Etiquette & Some Suggestions

Mannerisms in the Netherlands tend to be quite courteous, and introductions are an important part of any gathering. Conversation should be kept impersonal, as the Dutch are often rather reserved concerning personal subjects. Environmental awareness is an important part of the Dutch lifestyle, and the country spends twice the percentage of their gross domestic product on the environment as does the US, so speaking in any manner that may be construed as environmentally unfriendly is inadvisable. Spontaneity is often not appreciated—it is seen as being overly zealous. Business meetings should be arranged in advance, and attended with punctuality. Organization is important to the Dutch. Invitations to dine out will usually be accompanied by pre-dinner drinks at the hosts home before continuing to the restaurant. For businessmen, dark conservative business suits are the rule, but summer light-weight suits and lighter colors are becoming more popular. A raincoat and umbrella are necessities, and a jacket should be taken because even summer evenings may become nippy.

An annoying practice to some residents of the Netherlands is that of referring to the entire country as *Holland.* North and South Holland are but two provinces on the country's western coast—there are ten other provinces. Call the country *the Netherlands,* especially when speaking with the Dutch.

Portugal

Official Name:	**A República Portuguesa**
	(The Portuguese Republic)
Population:	**9.8 million**
Population Density:	**275 persons / mile² (106 /km²)**
Language:	**Portuguese (official)**
Currency Unit:	**Escudo (recently 153 escudo = $1)**
Area:	**35,516 miles², (91,981 km²)**
	—slightly smaller than Indiana
Form of Government:	**Republic**
Capital:	**Lisbon (Lisboa)**

Acts in the 15th century by Portuguese explorers, such as Vasco de Gama navigating the Cape of Good Hope and Magellan sailing much of the formerly unnavigated world, have led to the era being termed the Portuguese Age of Discovery. That era was propelled by a wealthy Portuguese kingdom, which led the world in exploration and colonialism throughout the Middle Ages. But two major catastrophes devastated the Portuguese empire: an earthquake in 1775 and Napoleon's invasion in 1807. The country has never fully recovered.

Since those setbacks, Portugal's membership in the European Community is likely the most significant event in the country's history. It is certainly the most encouraging and has aroused great hopes of a prosperous future.

Portugal's 20th century history has been marked by turmoil and instability. In 1910, the then in power monarchy was violently overthrown and replaced with a fledgling republic, only to be subsequently overthrown by a military takeover in 1926. During the period from 1932 to 1968, the country was ruled by a strong handed military dictator, Antonio Salazar, whose paternalistic methods gave stability to Portugal, but only at great cost, both moral and economic. The removal of the notorious bureaucracy produced by petty officials during the Salazar period remains one of the most important tasks Portugal must accomplish to assure success in the Single Market. On April 25, 1974, a bloodless coup was successful, and the victorious left-wing military leaders immediately put in place a Marxist government, which was decisively rejected by the people through elections held in 1976. After the elections, civilian rule was restored and Portugal effected a transition from dictatorship to democracy that enabled it to enter the EC along with Spain in 1986.

Government

The Portuguese government consists of an executive president, elected by the people for a five-year term, and an Assembly, also directly elected and having 250 members. Members of the Assembly are elected for four-year terms. The president appoints a prime minister, who commands a majority of the Assembly. The prime minister, in turn, appoints a Council of Ministers (Cabinet), which is responsible to the Assembly. Major political parties include the Social Democratic Party (PSD), the Socialist Party (PS), the center-left Democratic Renewal Party (PRD), the center-right Center Democratic Party (CDS), and the Communist Party (PCP). The Portuguese autonomous regions of Madeira and the Azores have their own independent governments.

The Economy

Though Portugal is the poorest country in the EC, it is wholly dedicated to the single-market program and to expanding its role in Community trade. It stands to gain greatly from a prosperous and united Europe. Portugal's 10 million people are mostly concentrated along the Atlantic coast in the cities of Lisbon (*Lisboa*), in the south (1 million people), and Oporto in the north (750,000 people). Other important industrial cities are Aveiro (wood products, engines and footwear); Coimbra (food products, textiles and chemicals) and Setubal (fish canning, automotive products, cement and metallurgy).

Portugal has had serious unemployment problems in past years, but the people are generally highly motivated and capable. In recent years, the unemployment problem has been significantly alleviated due to large investments by foreign companies wishing to tap Portugal's inexpensive labor market. The Portuguese have great expectations of their association with the European Community. They understand Portugal's lower production costs and wish to use this advantage to propel the country's languishing economy. Portugal's infrastructure—transportation, telephone, power distribution, etc.—still lags far behind the visions of the country's inhabitants, but it is improving steadily.

Although democracy has begun to distribute business influence in Portugal more evenly, the brunt of it is still held by 13 dominant families. The wealthy still hold a distinct advantage over others, through their access to the better private education system.

Customs, Protocols, Etiquette & Some Suggestions

Despite its poverty, the Portuguese are very proud of their heritage and are sincere, friendly, hospitable people. They are less temperamental than their Spanish neighbors and are always courteous. Overall, the atmosphere is extremely tranquil, almost drowsy, but the people of Portugal are hard workers who possess strong desires to improve the conditions in their country. They are very polite, and many attitudes remain quite formal. A great deal of pride is taken in personal appearance and this should be replicated when visiting their country.

Portugal has had a long history of trading with Europe and as such has more in common with many of the other European nations than it does with Spain. Do not mentally lump the two Iberian nations together—Portugal is quite different than Spain.

Most businesses close between noon and 3:00 pm, so arrange your affairs around these hours. Although a traditional business clothing is quite acceptable, Lisbon and the rest of the country have become quite casual (not tacky) often shunning ties in favor of an open-necked shirt. The weather in Portugal is generally warm and the thermometer rarely dips below freezing, even in winter.

Spain

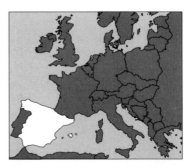

Official Name:	**España (Spain)**
Population:	**39 million**
Population Density:	**200 persons / mile² (77 /km²)**
Language(s):	**Spanish or Castilian (official; spoken as a first language by 71%), Catalan (as a first language 21%), Basque (3%), Galician (4%)**
Currency Unit:	**Peseta (recently 123 peseta = $1)**
Area:	**194,885 miles², (504,722 km²)**
	—slightly more than twice the size of Oregon
Form of Government:	**Constitutional Monarchy**
Capital:	**Madrid**

Spain, often naively associated only with bull fights and conquistadors, is actually a thoroughly diverse country that defies such generalizations. Modern Spain dates from the 1490s, a decade in which two important events took place: Columbus discovered America and established a great Spanish empire there, and the kingdom of the Moors, centered in Granada, was conquered, making Spain's territory on the Iberian peninsula complete, as it remains today.

In the 16th century, Spain was the greatest country in Europe. Gold and silver brought back by the conquistadors also made Spain one of Europe's wealthiest nations. Spain played a considerable part in European politics in the 18th century, until domination by Napoleon culminated a century of gradual decline.

The 19th century saw Spain withdraw from its involvement in northern European politics and regionalist movements, generally by the working class, began to define the political climate in the country. Cuba and the Philippine Islands were lost after the Spanish-American war with the USA in 1898. During World War I, Spain remained neutral, but the period was marked by significant political unrest internally. Increasing domestic strife and general political disorder led to the rise of the Spanish Fascist Party. In 1936, Spanish civil war broke out, ultimately to be won by General Francisco Franco's Nationalist forces in 1936. Following the civil war, neo-Fascist government ensued and from 1942 to 1967, political expression, not within the narrow band of acceptability as defined by the government, was prohibited. Additionally, the national parliament was not directly elected and the voice of the people had little to do with the way the country was run.

Spain remained neutral during World War II, although it was beheld by Germany. After World War II, General Franco emphasized that Spain's government would pursue anti-communist policies. This stance brought some international acceptance from Western nations during the Cold War. In 1969, Franco named Juan Carlos, grandson of Alfonso XIII (King of Spain from 1886-1931), his successor. When Franco died in 1975, the new King of Spain, Juan Carlos, initiated a new liberal constitution that has done a commendable job of transforming the country into a democracy. In 1982, Spain joined NATO and elected a socialist government and in 1986, Spain joined the EC, which represents a critical point in its effort to join main stream Europe.

Government

When Franco's dictatorship ended in 1975, it marked the end of the last dictatorship in Western Europe. The Spanish government today is a constitutional monarchy consisting of the King, a prime minister and a Parliament.

The Parliament is called the *Cortes* and consists of a Senate (Upper House) and a Chamber of Deputies (Lower House). The Senate consists of 208 senators—four from each province, five from the Balearic Islands, six from the Canary Islands and two each from Ceuta and Melilla. All are elected for four-year terms. In addition, 49 senators are indirectly elected by Spain's 17 autonomous regions. The Chamber of deputies has 350 members who are directly elected for four-year terms.

The King appoints a prime minister, who leads the *Cortes.* The prime minister then appoints a Council of Ministers, or Cabinet, who are responsible to the Chamber of Deputies. Each of the 17 regions has its own legislature.

The Economy

Spain has done well since joining the European Community in 1986. With increases in real gross national product (GNP) of around 5% each year since 1986, Spain has been the fastest growing member in the Community. Increased investment, both domestic and foreign, has been the most important factor pushing the economic expansion. The country's comparatively low salaries have attracted major investments from both European and foreign companies. Inflation was reduced to 4.8% in 1988, but the simmering economy has caused it to again become a problem. A war against inflation is being ardently fought by the Spanish government, who is concerned that rising prices and rocketing wages will cause Spanish goods and services to loose their advantage. Unemployment has steadily worsened over the past few years and is currently the worst in the Community with 1993 estimates of 21.5%.

Spain has been the grateful recipient of billions of ECUs in economic aid from the Community and is gradually improving its infrastructure and economic position. In 1992, Spain hosted the Summer Olympic Games in Barcelona and the Universal Exhibition in Seville, demonstrating both its ability and desire to show the world it has abandoned the isolationist policies of the Franco years.

Customs, Protocols, Etiquette & Some Suggestions

Traditionally, the image of Spaniards is one associated with the word *mañana*, which literally means "tomorrow," but really means "sometime" or "never". This image of easy going procrastination may have once typified the majority of Spaniards, but today it is being replaced by growing political concern and business activity.

Most of the EC countries have regional dissimilarities, but in Spain they are, perhaps, the most pronounced. In many ways, Spain cannot really be treated as one country. The Catalonians, the Basques, and the Andalusians strongly differ from each other, having contrasting cultures, tastes and business styles. In general, it is true to say that Spaniards are proud people, sometimes to the point of appearing pretentious, but this is balanced by their hospitality and generosity, which is among the world's best. The Spanish consider "honor" very important and a formal, almost ceremonial, attitude is reflected in their behavior, particularly in business. One sweeping feature of Spaniards, though, is great pride in their families, especially children.

Dinners in Spain tend to be taken very late—generally after 10:00 pm. If invited to dinner at a restaurant, it is polite to offer to pay, but accept that your host will probably insist that he be allowed to treat you. When being entertained at a Spaniard's home, it is not customary to bring gifts for the host or hostess. You should never break this tradition, though it is acceptable to later send a thank-you card or flowers to the lady of the house in appreciation of her hospitality. Gifts are, however, an accepted, almost expected, part of conducting business in Spain. Lastly, in business circles a dark, stylish suit is the accepted norm.

United Kingdom

Key to Numbered Regions

England		Northern Ireland	
1	Bedfordshire	1	Antrim
2	Berkshire	2	Ards
3	Buckinghamshire	3	Armagh
4	Greater London	4	Ballymena
5	Greater Manchester	5	Ballymoney
6	Hereford and	6	Banbridge
	Worcester	7	Belfast
7	Mid Glamorgan	8	Carrickfergus
8	Northamptonshire	9	Castlereagh
9	Nottinghamshire	10	Coleraine
10	South Glamorgan	11	Cookstown
11	South Yorkshire	12	Craigavon
12	Staffordshire	13	Down
13	Warwickshire	14	Dungannon
14	West Glamorgan	15	Fermanagh
15	West Midlands	16	Larne
16	West Yorkshire	17	Limavady
		18	Lisburn
		19	Londonderry
		20	Magherafelt
		21	Moyle
		22	Newry and Mourne
		23	Newtownabbey
		24	North Down
		25	Omagh
		26	Strabane

Official Name:	**United Kingdom of Great Britain and Northern Ireland**
Population:	**57.2 million**
Population Density:	**610 persons / mile^2 (236 /km^2)**
Language(s):	**English (official), Welsh and some Gaelic**
Currency Unit:	**British Pound (recently £1.5 = $1)**
Area:	**93,629 miles^2, (242,485 km^2) —a little smaller than Oregon**
Form of Government:	**Constitutional Monarchy**
Capital:	**London**

The United Kingdom (UK) is an island nation located in the northwest portion of the European continent. Its history has been heavily influenced by this strategic position. In the earliest centuries of this era, the area was a northwestern outpost of the Roman Empire, surrounded by walls to subdue warring Celtic tribes. It was eventually taken over by seafaring Germanic tribes and, later, missionaries from continental Europe managed to Christianize the newly conquered lands. The new Christians fought off wave after wave of onslaught by Germanic tribes, only to eventually fall to the Normans. This battle-filled, victor-and-vanquished manner fills the pages of Britain's history. Each group that came to the isles disordered, refigured and uniquely molded the UK's culture into what it is today. Celts, Danes, Saxons, Angles, Scots, Welsh, Flemings, Normans, Irish, Indians, Jews, Africans, West Indians and Pakistanis have all donated to creating the people of today's United Kingdom.

There may exist some confusion about the relationship and differences between the *United Kingdom, Great Britain, Britain,* and *England.* Great Britain and Britain are synonymous and are defined as the combined area of England, Wales and Scotland, which together comprise the island of Great Britain. England comprises the southern most two-thirds of the island, Scotland the northern most third and Wales is positioned to the west of England. The United Kingdom is defined as Great Britain plus Northern Ireland (the southern part of Ireland is, of course, an independent member nation of the EC). Finally, to avoid confusion, it should be mentioned that *Britannia* is the name given to the personification of Britain. It is shown as a woman with a shield, helmet and trident.

Government

The government of the United Kingdom is a constitutional monarchy, without a written constitution. The UK's Parliament consists of two houses, the upper House of Lords and the lower House of Commons. The House of Lords consists of 750 non-elected, hereditary peers and peeresses. It is composed of some 20 Lords of Appeal, over 370 life peers, and two archbishops and 24 bishops of the Church of England. The House of Commons contains 650 members who are elected by the populace under a system of proportional representation for five-year terms. The current sovereign is Her Majesty Queen Elizabeth II, who took the position upon the death of her father on February 6, 1952. The sovereign appoints a prime minister who commands a majority in the House of Commons. The predominant political parties are currently the Conservative Party and the Labor Party. Other parties include the Liberal Democrats and various regional parties including the Scottish National Party, the (Welsh Nationalist) Plaid Cymru, the Ulster Unionists, the Democratic Unionist Party, and the (Northern Ireland) Social Democratic and Labour Party.

The Economy

Though its has fallen from the lofty levels of bygone eras, the UK is still one of the world's great trading powers and financial centers. Its economy is among the largest in Europe. Whether it is the fourth or fifth largest in Europe is a topic of debate—recently Italy shocked the British by claiming they had surpassed Britain as the world's fourth largest economy.

Britain's economy is essentially capitalistic, but has historically had a generous mixture of social welfare programs and government ownership. Over the last decade the government has virtually stopped the expansion of welfare measures and has promoted extensive privatization of many state run facilities. Britain is, by far, the most popular country for US companies who wish to enter the European market, but Japanese firms also have a very high level of investment in Britain.

Agriculture is highly mechanized and efficient by European standards, producing about 60% of the UK's food while utilizing only 1% of the labor force. Industrial companies, both public and private, employ about 24% of the work force and generate 22% of the country's gross domestic product. The UK is an energy-rich nation with large coal, natural gas, and oil reserves.

Following the recession of 1979-81, the economy enjoyed the longest period of continuous economic growth it has had in the last 30 years. During the period of 1982-89, real GDP grew by about 25%, while the inflation rate of 14% was nearly halved. Between 1986 and 1989, unemployment fell from 11% to about 6%. But by the end of the 1980s and beginning of the 1990s, inflation became a major problem and interest rates soared. Britain's growth rate went from one of Europe's highest, to one of Europe's lowest. By 1992, inflation had again been brought under control, but the constraints of the ERM forced British officials to keep interest rates high, keeping the British economy from resuming the growth it had enjoyed in the 1980s. Following its withdrawal from the ERM in September 1992, interest rates were lowered and Britain's economy has slowly but surely strengthened. Unemployment, estimated to average 11.5% in 1993, is slowly coming down. Despite being cautious supporters of the EC, British officials have made it clear that they are in no hurry to rejoin the ERM and will not consider it until the recent recovery seems enduring.

Customs, Protocols, Etiquette & Some Suggestions

The United Kingdom is one of the most enchanting places for an American to visit because the British, though they speak the same language and have closer ties to the USA than other European countries, still seem somehow wonderfully different and are curiously addictive. Though Americans may be intrigued by the British, it must be said that the British are equally intrigued by Americans.

In general, the English are extraordinarily polite and reserved—waiting their turn in line even if it means missing the bus. But once they open up, they are gifted conversationalists (i.e., chatty) and can make brilliant conversation out of even the flimsiest material. Though the world knows relatively little about the Welsh (except that their language sounds funny) and the Scots (aside from kilts and bagpipes), they too are a likable bunch. It is a British custom, more than in many other countries, to extend invitations to their homes. If invited, take advantage of the opportunity and enjoy your host's generosity. It would be appropriate to send a thank-you card the following day and perhaps present a gift of chocolate or wine upon arrival.

Business transactions with Britons require punctuality, politeness, initial formality and sincerity. Dress should be conservative, yet tasteful. Unlike other Europeans, the British tend to shake hands only at first meetings, or after a long absence—beyond these circumstances, hand shaking is not necessary.

8

The "Other Europe" - the European Free Trade Association

Honest differences are often a healthy sign of progress.

— Mahatma Gandhi

After the European Economic Community was created in 1957, attempts were made to coordinate the six members of the EC with the majority of the remaining Western European nations. The proposed arrangement would have formed a giant, 17-member free-trade area, but the negotiations ultimately failed. The failure was caused partly by EC fears that the integrity of their association would be impaired by the suggested plan, and partly due to other nations' concerns.

Regardless of the cause, the breakdown of the negotiations left many Western European nations outside the EC. Fear, about being excluded from the process of European integration and prejudiced economically by the deregulated EC member states, caused concern about the economic challenge the EC represented. In response to these anxieties, negotiations rapidly ensued between many non-EC nations to create a free-trade organization of their own. On January 4, 1960, Great Britain, Switzerland, Austria, Portugal, Denmark, Sweden, and Norway signed a convention in Stockholm Sweden that established the European Free Trade Association (EFTA).

Economic concerns, however, were not the only motive for establishing EFTA. Differing views regarding the concept of European cooperation existed then, as they do today, and EFTA represented an alternative for those countries who were not in complete agreement with the goals held by the EC. During the past 50 years, two basic concepts concerning European integration have existed. The first is based on the idea of building a united Europe in which not only are the member nation's economies integrated, but their political and social policies are as well. This is the approach largely taken by the EC, particularly in view of the Treaty of Maastricht, which would, if ratified, add a social charter to the Treaty of Rome. The second approach, the one adopted by the member countries of EFTA, consists of a purely commercial association whose purpose is only to facilitate the exchange of goods through the removal of customs barriers and differing technical standards. These dissenting points of view regarding European integration explain why two different organizations, each having a primary goal of facilitating international economic cooperation in Western Europe, developed side by side.

Although EFTA was founded as a reaction to the creation of the EEC, it was never intended to be its rival. EFTA's founding document, the Convention of Stockholm, says explicitly that one of EFTA's fundamental purposes is to eliminate trade barriers between the EEC countries and EFTA. Today, EFTA consists of Switzerland, Austria, Finland, Iceland, Norway, Sweden and Liechtenstein. It is a much smaller organization than the European Community, with a total population of just under 32 million (versus about 340 million in the EC). The population of each EFTA member nation is shown below.

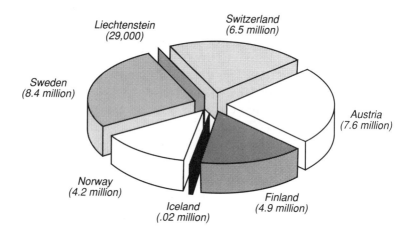

Population of the EFTA Nations

Operation of EFTA

Unlike the EC, EFTA possesses neither supranational authority nor institutions. EFTA has a Council that serves as its directing body and is headquartered in Geneva, Switzerland. The Council is composed of either permanent representatives who are delegated by the member countries to Geneva, or of the actual foreign ministers of the seven member nations. The permanent representatives meet approximately twice a month, while the actual foreign ministers assemble only about twice per year. The decisions made by the Council are generally agreed to unanimously. A majority vote system exists, but is rarely used. EFTA has an annual budget of approximately $10.5 million.

History of EFTA

1960   Switzerland, Austria, Sweden, Denmark, Norway, Portugal and the United Kingdom signed the treaty establishing the European Free Trade Association.

1961   Finland joined the European Free Trade Association.

1966   EFTA eliminated all customs controls on industrial products between its member states.

1970   Iceland joined the European Free Trade Association as an "associate member."

1972   The countries of EFTA and those of the EEC completed agreements for free trade between themselves that were strictly limited to commercial matters and included very general principles for competition conditions.

1973   The United Kingdom and Denmark withdrew from EFTA to join the EEC.

1976   EFTA established a fund of $100 million for the development of Portugal.

1984   On April 9, 1984, a meeting between the ministers of the EC Commission and EFTA was held in Luxembourg at which it was decided to intensify the cooperation between the two organizations with an ultimate goal of creating a "European Economic Space" (EES) in Western Europe.

1985   The ministers of the EC Commission and those of EFTA decided to begin meeting regularly.

1986   Portugal left EFTA to join the EEC. Iceland's "associate member" status was upgraded to make Iceland a full member.

1989   Jacques Delors made a proposal to the European Parliament to begin negotiations to create a European Economic Area (EEA) between the EC and EFTA.

1990   Formal negotiations between the EC and EFTA began toward the establishment of the European Economic Area, which would essentially extend the benefits of the 1992 single-market program to the countries of EFTA.

1991   Liechtenstein joined EFTA as a full member, completing EFTA's present seven nation membership of Switzerland, Austria, Sweden, Norway, Finland, Iceland and Liechtenstein.

In its 31 years of existence, EFTA has served its member countries satisfactorily. It was successful in attaining a free-trade zone of industrial products within its borders, and has been able to create a bridge between its members and the members of the EC. Since its founding, three original members have left EFTA to join the EC: Great Britain, Portugal and Denmark. Meanwhile, three new members, Finland, Iceland and Liechtenstein, have joined EFTA. The agreements made in 1972 for free trade between the EEC and EFTA have had a two-sided positive effect. They created the bridge between the two zones of economic integration in Western Europe and they made it possible to maintain free trade between the countries who have remained members of EFTA and those who have left it to join the EC. Since the agreement in 1972 between the EC and EFTA, the relationship between the two organizations has developed progressively.

During the 1960s, EFTA was successful at keeping up with the EEC simply by adopting similar tariff reductions as those implemented by the Community. This tactic, however, has become less effective over time. The advent of the Single Market has outdated the "parallel tariff reduction strategy" entirely because the 1992 Internal Market program entails broad legislative aspects that cannot be easily duplicated within EFTA. As both are quite aware, the EC and EFTA are important to each other. Each is the others major trading partner, with 55.9% (1988) of all EFTA exports going to EC countries, and 26.5% (1987) of all EC exports going to EFTA countries. It is impossible for the two organizations to ignore each other, and the well-being of one depends heavily upon the well-being of the other. Because of this interdependence, it is in the best interest of both organizations that something be done to prevent EFTA from becoming alienated by the EC's single-market program.

Presently, three choices exist for EFTA member countries. The first is to do nothing—a choice that would undoubtedly result in hazardous economic isolation. The second is to seek membership with the EC itself, effectively abandoning EFTA as a relic that served its owners well for many years, but is no longer up to the task. Requests for commencement of negotiations toward joining the EC have already been made by Austria, Finland, Sweden and Switzerland, and more EFTA countries may follow. In the mean time, the third and most palatable option to many EFTA countries is progressing through negotiations with the EC regarding the establishment of a 19 country free-trade area known as the European Economic Area (EEA). The EEA (formally referred to as the EES, European Economic Space) will include all the countries of the EC and EFTA and will serve as the vital addition necessary to EFTA's framework to keep it from being left out of the European Single Market. For those EFTA countries wishing to join the EC, the EEA will serve as an excellent stepping stone toward making the transition.

The European Economic Area (EEA)

The EC and the countries of EFTA began formal negotiations toward the establishment of the European Economic Area in June 1990. These negotiations were intended to fill three essential purposes:

1) To offer to the countries of EFTA the most complete, unbiased access possible to the EC's Single Market. This implies participation of the EFTA countries in the four basic freedoms guaranteed by the Common Market—the free movement of goods, services, capital

and people. In exchange, the markets of the EFTA countries will be open to all the countries of the EEA.

2) The second objective is to intensify cooperation in related political areas, such as research and development, education, environmental protection, consumer protection, etc.

3) Finally, the EEA seeks to diminish the economic and social differences, (for example average wage for a class of workers and standard number of hours in a work week) between its member countries.

The European Economic Area will allow the EFTA countries to participate in the EC's Single Market at terms closely similar to those of an EC member country. Free transit of goods, services, capital and persons will be assured to the same extent as between EC member states.

The difference between the EEA status and full EC membership is that while the participation of non-EC member states, in economic terms, is virtually the same as EC member states, participation at the institutional level is vastly different. In contrast to EC member states, non-EC member states involved in the EEA will not be allowed to participate fully in the decision making process and in administrative proceedings concerning the integrated EC market. The non-EC member states will be forced to assume a sideline role because the preeminent role in the decision making realm is assigned to the EC by the EEA Treaty. Additionally, the two-pillared institutional structure of the EEA (on one hand the EC, on the other the EFTA countries) creates an atmosphere that automatically gives precedence to the EC institutions.

The EEA treaty was jeopardized when Switzerland rejected it in December 1992. The remaining six EFTA nations continued the negotiations, however, and overcame serious EC reservations by agreeing to pay 60% of the financial contribution that would have been paid by the Swiss. The money will go to a "cohesion" fund, which will primarily benefit the EC's poorest nations—Greece, Spain, Portugal and Ireland.

Of all the EFTA nations, only Iceland has not applied to join the European Community (though Switzerland's application is currently on hold since the EEA was rejected by Swiss voters). Thus, since Sweden, Norway, Finland, and Austria all hope to become members of the EC by January 1995, the EEA may be a short-lived organization.

In addition to the member countries of EFTA, the EEA envisions eventual association with the emerging democratic countries of Eastern Europe. Some facets of this are explored in the following chapter.

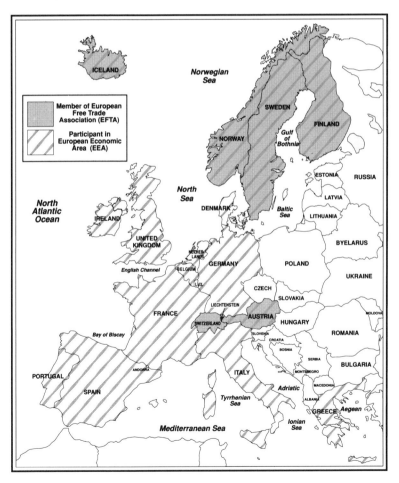

The European Economic Area

9

Future Challenges

Life affords no higher pleasure than that of surmounting difficulties, passing from one step of success to another, forming new wishes and seeing them gratified.

—Samuel Johnson

The arrival of the 1992 single European market was supposed to bring with it economic prosperity and increased unity. Instead, Europe is presently in a state of disarray, and is enduring the worst economic slowdown of the decade. Its troubles are highlighted by the recession, controversy surrounding the Maastricht Treaty, rising nationalism and protectionism in many countries, currency turmoil, and a war in Yugoslavia raging just outside the EC's borders. There are many reasons for Europe's present state, but one of the prime causes is, ironically, the collapse of Communism.

The demise of the Soviet Union created incredible strains on the EC. The reunification of Germany forced the German Bundesbank to keep interest rates abnormally high, forcing the other member states to adopt economy-stifling policies at a moment when they could least afford to do so. This led the Exchange Rate Mechanism into chaos, and is one of the foremost reasons for the EC's economic woes. After the UK dropped out of the ERM following the September 1992 currency crisis, its economy began to show signs of improvement almost immediately. This is not to argue that the other EC member states should also quit the ERM, but rather to show that when Germany is able to lower its interest rates, economic improvements across the EC are bound to follow.

Fear of an uncontrolled deluge of hungry, unemployed Easterners has led to a rise of ultra-right, anti-European parties in Germany, Italy and France. This is primarily because the Easterners are an ideal scapegoat who can be blamed for problems with which they have little to do. Unemployment in the EC, an issue that has long been recognized as being connected to Europe's fragmented markets, could be significantly reduced by removing artificial barriers between people, rather than creating them. The problems can be solved peacefully and intelligently—not through the violent and unsuccessful methods of the past.

Everything considered, the fall of Communism and the end of the Cold War must be regarded as nothing short of a miracle. The problems that are being left in its wake are obstacles whose removal will pave the way toward a better, safer, more comfortable world. Despite the problems in Europe now, it would be a mistake to say that the 1992 program has failed, or that European unity is an unobtainable dream. It is still likely that Europe will eventually adopt a single currency, expand to include most of the newly emerging democracies of Eastern Europe, and grow to compete with the United States and Japan—all without aid from trade restrictions or government subsidies. But this will not come easily. The future holds many difficult decisions for the European Community, and will likely bring changes to the way the EC operates.

The Change Toward More Democratic Accountability

The European Community is, and has always been, perceived in different ways by different people. There are essentially two broad schools of thought concerning what the EC should try to become. One is held by "federalists" in Europe, who want the Community to evolve into a kind of United States of Europe, in which a strong central government steers the Community from Brussels. The other is held by "Euro-skeptics" who insist that the EC ought to be no more than a loose confederation of nations who cooperate with each other, but only as sovereign nations who may refuse to participate whenever it becomes uncomfortable. Many people, of course, don't fully support either of the two extreme positions, but feel that the Community should fall somewhere in between.

Advances made by the EC so far, particularly for those of the federalist point of view, have been achieved without explicitly defining what the Community was meant to become. Federalists feared that announcing plans to create the "United States of Europe" would stir up paralyzing opposition and prevent anything from being accomplished. Instead, small but irreversible steps have gradually introduced federal ideas into the Community, sometimes tricking national parliaments who realized too late that some of their laws could be overturned by the European Court of Justice. But to some extent these methods have violated the fundamental rule of democracy to "govern with the consent of the governed." The role that the Community presently plays in Europe has been achieved largely without the consent or even the knowledge of its citizens. EC proposals have been implemented simply by gaining the acceptance of politicians without concern for the opinions of the people. Recent events, however, have shown that the citizens of the Community are no longer willing to accept this.

The French and Danish referendums on the treaty of Maastricht created an eye opener for EC politicians in this regard. In the French referendum, the Maastricht treaty was barely approved, with "yes" votes of just 51.05%. This result came only three months after the Danish rejected the treaty by 50.7%. Although a second referendum on the treaty won the Dane's approval (57% voted "yes"), the initial rejection reveals concerns that are held by many Europeans. One of the primary reasons given by citizens for casting a "no" vote, in both referendums, was simply that the citizen was unsure of what was contained in the treaty and how it would affect his or her daily life. The Maastricht treaty was written in highly technical language, and was never meant to be easily understood by the average citizen. It was carefully written to satisfy the politicians, reflecting a delicate balance between the Euro-skeptics and the federalists, but EC bureaucrats largely neglected to inform the Community's citizens of the effects of the treaty. As a result many French and Danish citizens concluded that it was safer to vote "no" to Maastricht than to send their nations down an unknown, possibly perilous path. This conclusion was reached even though opinion polls had shown that the majority of the EC's citizens support European Monetary Union. The saga of the Maastricht treaty serves to demonstrate the need to begin including EC citizens in the development of the Community. Without their support, it is unlikely that the EC will gain much ground in the coming years.

Expansion of the Community

Whether outside nations should be allowed to join the EC is presently one of the most difficult issues the Community must contend with, and controversy regarding expansion is likely to follow the Community far into the future. For the moment though, a consensus has been reached, agreeing that expansion should not be considered until the Maastricht treaty is ratified. This obstacle, however, will not remain in place perpetually, and the Community will eventually be forced to confront the expansion issue head-on. EC membership is a much sought after credential today, and recent events in Europe have made the queue of nations waiting to apply much longer than would have been possible only a few years ago. Nowhere has the old order changed so quickly since the demise of the Cold War as it has in Europe. Nations once firmly embraced within the confining arms of communism are now struggling democracies, hoping to join the EC and use it as a source of stability and guidance.

Before accepting new members, the EC's institutions and current member nations must confront the issue of whether the Community is ready and able to create the structures necessary to ensure political stability, security and wealth across an expanded territory. Clearly it would be foolish to attempt to take in all of Europe at once, so expansion will have to follow a carefully planned procedure. The timing and order of any expansion is critical. Currently, eight nations have applied for EC membership: Austria, Norway, Finland, Sweden, Switzerland, Malta, Cyprus and Turkey. Many others have implied that they would, one day, like to join the EC.

Expansion to Include the EFTA Nations

The EFTA countries are the most economically advanced of the applicants and will likely be the first to be accepted into the EC. As described in Chapter 8, the members of EFTA will be able to enjoy the economic virtues of the single market even without becoming EC members through the European Economic Area (EEA) agreement. The EEA agreement, however, is not strong enough in itself to dissuade members of EFTA from seeking full membership in the EC. Five of the seven EFTA nations have already applied for membership. The reasons the EFTA nations feel compelled to join the EC club when they already are able to benefit from the Single Market are diverse, but perhaps the strongest is that the EEA makes provisions only on economic terms, divorcing the EFTA nations from the Community's decision making process. In other words, the EFTA nations are bound by some 1,400 pages of EC laws, yet have no say regarding their content and they cannot change them. Only members of the EC may influence Community policy, providing strong motivation for the EFTA nations to seek EC membership.

Economically, the applicants from EFTA are ready to meet the membership obligations of the EC and would be net contributors to, not recipients of, the EC budget. This is because they are among Europe's wealthiest nations. Their help in sharing the burden of transferring wealth to the EC's poorer regions would be welcomed by all of the current members. The EFTA nations would find it easier to meet the convergence criteria for monetary union than some of the present members of the EC, and are long-established democracies that could make useful political contributions to the Community. As such, the admittance of the EFTA nations into the EC is widely viewed as a necessary first step toward admitting the former communist nations of Eastern Europe.

On May 26, 1992, the Federal Council of Switzerland submitted a request for negotiations regarding their entrance into the EC. Subsequently, Switzerland's voters rejected participation in the European Economic Area (EEA), putting Swiss plans to enter the EC under scrutiny. In spite of the nation not participating in the EEA, officials continue to discuss entering the Community and it is likely that one day the Swiss people will accept this change. Switzerland's willingness to join the EC was enhanced by the end of the Cold War because neutrality, an attribute cherished for decades by the Swiss, is no longer as delicate an issue.

In Finland, politicians and big business support the EC, but this was also the case in Denmark where a less enthusiastic Danish public shocked Europe by initially voting against the Treaty of Maastricht. A few years ago opinion polls in Finland showed a solid two-thirds public majority in favor of joining the EC. Now, public favor has diminished to the point that the majority is held by those against membership in the EC. One of the primary reasons for the Finnish change of heart is that if the nation becomes a member of the EC, it will contribute more money than it receives because its GNP is considerably higher than the Community average. This outflow of money to the EC didn't concern the Finnish a few years ago because Finland had one of the healthiest economies in the world. The tide has turned however, and Finland now finds itself in the worse economic slump it has seen since World War II. Unemployment, for example, was at an enviously low 1.3% in 1989, but 1993 finds the figure has skyrocketed to 18% and is rising.

The reason for Finland's economic distress is the same as its reason for applying to join the European Community: the demise of the Soviet Union. The failure of the USSR was a major misfortune to the economy of Finland. Trade with the former USSR accounted for over 20% of Finland's exports and provided a reliable, protected market that sheltered Finland from the austerities of the external world economy. The Finnish capital, Helsinki, was to the Soviet Union what Hong Kong is to China. It provided the USSR with a window to the West, and was an important part of East/West relations. Now, Finland has lost the majority of its influence and markets in the East and it finds itself simply a distant Nordic country on the northern fringes of Europe. Despite public opinion to the contrary, these circumstances have caused Finnish politicians and big businesses to see the wisdom in seeking association with the EC.

In the other EFTA nations, most government officials have high hopes of eventually joining the EC—every EFTA country, except Iceland, has applied. This enthusiasm, however, is not always shared by the populace. Switzerland's refusal of the EEA, and recent opinion poles in Norway showing strong aversion to joining the EC, demonstrate this fear of change.

Expansion to include the Nations of Eastern Europe

To two generations of EC citizens, the countries of eastern Europe were relatively unknown before the radical reforms of 1989. They were perceived as oppressed satellites of Russia with little separate identity of their own and a uniformly low standard of living. Great changes have taken place in the European environment since the Single European Act and the White Paper were first written. A wave of reform has swept through eastern Europe producing several new, enthusiastic, yet inexperienced democracies. The Soviet Union has crumbled and Germany has been reunited. As of yet, no new order has really emerged to replace the one that so rapidly came into being following World War II, making it likely that the young democracies of central and eastern Europe will face enormous economic difficulties.

The EC must decide what stance to take regarding these newly liberated countries. Many far-sighted diplomats believe that to avoid endless turmoil on the EC's eastern borders, eventually the former communist nations must be given the chance to deeply establish themselves in democratic Europe. Membership in the EC would be the ideal way to accomplish this.

Poland

Poland was the first of the Central and Eastern European countries to embark on a revolution to establish democratic rule. In 1989, public unrest and economic problems prevailed over the ruling Communist party and the first free elections were held resulting in a 24-member coalition government, of which only four seats were held by Communists.

Hungary

Hungary has been the most determined economic reformer in Eastern Europe, and was the first to clearly express its intention to seek entry into the EC as rapidly as possible.

Czechoslovakia

A series of powerful anti-Communist demonstrations led the party to effectively hand over power to the anti-Communist Civic Forum party. Unfortunately, tensions within the Czech and Slovak portions of the country have since forced it to divide and, as of January 31, 1992, Czechoslovakia no longer exists as a unified country. The tensions that divided the country were based on Slovak fears that their Czech compatriots would hoard decision making powers in the newly formed democracy and would look down on Slovaks as incapable siblings. Czech responses to the Slovak apprehensions did little to alleviate them. Whether the Czechs would really have attempted to subordinate the Slovaks if Czechoslovakia remained united is uncertain. Theorizing about what might have happened is of little use, however, as the country's leaders have already decided to split the country. This has left the Czechoslovakian people somewhat perplexed and confused by the logic of their leaders. Severe tensions do not really exist between the two groups of people. Over 70 years of living together had made them quite used to each other, and the fact that the country is now divided seems strange to many citizens.

In its former Communist days, Czechoslovakia had a stronger democratic tradition than any other Eastern European country. This, combined with it being the most industrially advanced former Communist bloc country, makes a future entry into the EC a less difficult proposition for former Czechoslovakia. It has a well-educated work force and is thought to be the ex-Soviet bloc country who is best placed to make the transaction to a market economy.

Bulgaria

Before the demise of the Soviet Union, Bulgaria's economy was closely integrated with the USSR's. Thus, the reform process will be more difficult than in some of its other Eastern European neighbors. Bulgaria was the only country where, after the establishment of a system of free elections, the former Communist party won a clear majority. Bulgaria currently faces very difficult problems with inefficiencies, shortages, corruption and a very ill economy. The poor state of the Bulgarian economy makes reform all the more difficult.

Romania

Romania is the country that is predicted to have the most difficult time restoring democratic institutions and political and economic stability. No other country in Eastern Europe had to endure the degree of oppression that was forced upon the Romanians. The country was impoverished by the harsh, corrupt and totalitarian rule of the Ceausescu regime that lasted from 1965 until 1989. In 1989, after the secret police violently put down demonstrators, an army-supported national revolt broke out. Nicolae Ceausescu and his wife were executed by a military tribunal on charges of genocide and corruption and most of the oppressive legislation put in place by his regime was annulled. The road toward success as measured by Western standards will be very long, and is only worsened by Romania's acute shortage of educated people to help achieve it.

Consequences of Expansion

When the EC does decide to expand, what will the consequences be? Talks have already begun that could expand the EC to 15 or 16 members by 1996. Since many of the EFTA nations would prefer to see the Community remain an organization of sovereign states, rather than become the "United States of Europe," one possible effect is that admittance of several EFTA nations may cause the momentum of the Community to sway in this direction.

Many Europeans are concerned that an enlarged EC will become unmanageable without major reforms. They doubt that the current legislative system will function efficiently with additional members. More members will make the EC more difficult to manage for many reasons. Among them:

- Unanimous decisions will be even harder to obtain. Although decisions may be reached by majority vote for proposals concerning the "single market," unanimity is still required in matters concerning taxation, energy, some environmental matters and other critical issues. If all the member states are unable to agree on a proposal, the result is often gridlock and zero progress—regardless of the importance of the issue.

- The Maastricht treaty calls for a common foreign and security policy, but relies entirely on the voluntary cooperation of the member states. The EFTA nations have a proud history of neutrality and may be reluctant to allow the EC to create a truly unified defense and foreign policy. This would force the EC to remain as it is now—a mighty economic force with only marginal foreign policy powers.

- EC Council meetings will become lengthy and difficult to orchestrate. Presently, each minister is allowed to make an introductory speech at Council meetings before actually proceeding to the meeting's true agenda. With 16 or more members, Council meetings would very likely grow to unbearable length if this practice were to continue. Furthermore, voting—especially majority voting where each member state is assigned a number of votes based roughly on its population—will become more complex. Currently, the weightings are such that one large country and three small nations can reject a proposal. Some EC officials are concerned that the addition of four or more small countries may alter the majority-vote balance such that it would be easier for a group of small countries to defeat a measure. This, it is feared, would give small nations power grossly disproportionate to their populations and might adversely affect the credibility of EC decisions.

- The Commission would face uncomfortable changes. Many feel that, with 17 members, the Commission is already to large. If the Community were to expand, the new members would surely insist that they too be able to appoint Commission representatives, adding to the Commission's size and complexity.

- The system of rotating presidencies will become more complicated. Under the present system, as discussed in Chapter 4, the member states rotate alphabetically through terms serving as president of the Council. The terms last six months and the nation holding the presidency sets the Council's agenda during that period. Even with the current 12 members, this system provides little continuity and with 16, each member nation would have to wait eight years between presidencies. Furthermore, the EC often uses a system of past, present and next presidencies to assemble a group to serve as an EC envoy. There is an understandable fear that the EC would be ridiculed if it sent a delegation from, say, Lithuania, Luxembourg and Malta to a crisis somewhere in the world.

- A larger European Parliament may likely be a weaker rather than stronger organization. The present 518 members of the European Parliament will increase to

567 in 1994 as a result of the reunification of Germany and other population shifts. The addition of new member states would make the size of the Parliament grow to 800, 900,1000 or even more members, further amplifying the already loud call for additional Parliamentary powers. These cries are sure to be resisted by the various national parliaments as they grow concerned over their future relevance, causing even more strife.

- More member states will mean more languages. The EC already has nine official languages, and requires an enormous staff simply to manage the tasks of translation and interpretation.

***

These difficult issues will provide plenty for EC politicians to grapple with in the future. But if the "ever closer union" called for by the Maastricht Treaty is to be achieved, ways must be found to reach basic agreements on each question. It will not be an easy task ... yet nobody ever said keeping nearly a half-billion people in peace and prosperity was easy. It is, though, deeply worthwhile.

Additional Sources of Information

The following addresses are official EC offices that can provide a wealth of additional information on the EC, often at no cost. A free catalog may be obtained from any of these offices entitled "The European Community as a Publisher." It lists books and other sources of information that are capable of answering virtually any question concerning the Community.

United States

Washington, D.C.

Commission of the European Communities
2100 M Street, NW
Suite 707
Washington, DC 20037
USA
Tel. (202) 862 9500

New York

Commission of the European Communities
3 Dag Hammarskjöld Plaza
305 East 47th Street
New York, NY 10017
USA
Tel. (212) 371 3804

United Kingdom

England

Commission of the European Communities
Jean Monnet House
8 Storey's Gate
London SW1P 3AT
United Kingdom
Tel. 222 81 22

Northern Ireland

Commission of the European Communities
Windsor House
9/15 Bedford Street
Belfast BT2 7EG
United Kingdom
Tel. 240 708

Wales

Commission of the European Communities
4 Cathedral Road
PO Box 15
Cardiff CF1 9SG
United Kingdom
Tel. 37 16 31

Scotland

Commission of the European Communities
9 Alva Street
Edinburgh EH2 4PH
United Kingdom
Tel. 225 20 58

Ireland

Commission of the European Communities
Jean Monnet Centre
39 Molesworth Street
Dublin 2
Republic of Ireland
Tel. 71 22 44

Luxembourg

Office for Official Publications of the European Communities
2, rue Mercier
L-2985 Luxembourg
Tel. 499 28 1

Chronology of the EC

1950   Robert Schuman, the foreign minister of France, proposes to form a coalition, initially with Germany, to manage the production of coal and steel.

1951   Treaty of Paris signed, creating the European Coal and Steel Community.

1955   The Six members of the ECSC meet in Messina, Italy, in an attempt to further their efforts toward increasing European cooperation.

1957   Treaties are signed in Rome that create the European Economic Community (EEC) and the European Atomic Energy Community (Euratom).

1960   The European Free Trade Association (EFTA) is founded.

1962   The United Kingdom applies for EC membership only two years after the formation of the EFTA, but is rejected, primarily because of objections from France's president, Charles de Gaulle.

1967   The merger treaty signed in Brussels in 1965 comes into force, replacing the three separate Councils and Commissions of the ECSC, the EEC, and Euratom with a single Council and a single Commission. The European Parliament and the Court of Justice remain common to the three Communities (ECSC, EEC, Euratom).

1967   Value-added taxes (VAT) are introduced in the six then member states of the Community.

1968   The EC establishes a Customs Union that eliminates duties at borders and sets a common tariff.

1970   The Werner Report is published, providing the primary blueprint for European monetary integration.

1970   The United Kingdom reapplies for membership in the EEC. Applications for membership are also accepted from Norway, Denmark and Ireland.

1972   An exchange mechanism known as the "Snake" is set up to stabilize currency fluctuations in the EC.

1973-1984   Period of "Eurosclerosis". Though the Community is expanded with the addition of 6 new member states and some important legislation is introduced, this period marks a definite slowdown of progress toward the "single market" goal of the Treaty of Rome. This period sees a resurgence of protectionist legislation from member states which effectively replaces the tariffs removed in the late 1960's. There is continual intra-country bickering caused by a lack of common ambitions, and the EC remains somewhat stagnate until the Single European Act is introduced in 1985.

1973 The United Kingdom, Denmark and Ireland are allowed admission into the EEC. Norway is forced to remove its application from consideration, due to the results of a referendum which show 53% of the voting population against Norway's EC membership. The EC 6 becomes the EC 9.

1975 The European Regional Development Fund is set up to provide money to help the less developed Member Nations of the EC improve their infrastructure.

1979 The European Monetary System (EMS) is initiated. Its primary objective is to create currency stability within the European Community. The European Currency Unit (ECU) is also introduced in this year as the "European currency".

1979 The European Parliament is elected by direct vote of European citizens for the first time.

1981 Greece joins the European Community, bringing the total number of Member Nations in the EC to 10.

1985 In June 1985, the Commission publishes a paper detailing a plan to create a single market by the end of 1992. The paper is called "Completing the Internal Market: White Paper from the Commission to the European Council," or simply, the "White Paper." In December 1985, the Single European Act, which allows more decisions to be made by majority vote instead of unanimity, is agreed upon.

1986 Portugal and Spain enter the EC, bringing the total number of member nations to 12, where it remains today.

1987 The Single European Act enters force. This act, officially entitled "The Single Act: A new frontier for Europe," is based on the guidelines established in the White Paper and sets out the general reforms necessary to establish a single market by January 1993, and requires member nations to bring their laws into accordance with those of the EC.

1988 The European Council instructs a committee chaired by Commission President Jacques Delors to suggest a methodology toward achieving economic and monetary union in the EC.

1989 After 10 months of effort, the committee chaired by Delors presents its findings in a report entitled 'Report on economic and monetary union in the European Community'. It details, in three stages, a procedure to realize economic and monetary union. It also points out that the Treaty of

Rome does not have the capacity for such an objective, thereby making a treaty change (followed by the necessary changes in national laws) mandatory if economic and monetary union is to become a reality.

1990   The United Kingdom becomes a full member of the European Monetary System after years of hesitation.

1990   Negotiations with the countries of the European Free Trade Association (EFTA) commence with the desire to create a European Economic Area by extending a majority of the provisions of the Single Market to cover EFTA.

1990   The Schengen Convention is signed by Belgium, France, Germany, Luxembourg and the Netherlands. The convention eliminates border controls for travelers between the five countries beginning January, 1991 and provides an excellent prototype for the larger removal of controls mandated by the Single Act to begin a year later. Afterward, Italy, Spain and Portugal also joined the convention. Border controls are maintained for non-EC residents.

1991   A summit is convened in Maastricht, Netherlands, and the necessary treaty is established which would amend the Treaty of Rome to allow economic and monetary union, as well as various political and social union, to materialize. Members of the Summit agreed to have a single currency and European Central Bank by no later than 1999.

1992   Greece and Luxembourg ratify Treaty of Maastricht in their parliaments.

1992   In June 1992, the Treaty of Maastricht is rejected by Denmark's voters in a national referendum—51% voted against the treaty. Ireland approves the treaty by 69%.

1992   In September 1992, France's voters narrowly approved the Maastricht treaty.

1992   The September 16, 1992 currency crisis rocks Europe's financial markets. Chaotic trading in the currency markets leads the United Kingdom and Italy to indefinitely withdraw from the European Monetary System.

1993   On January 1, 1993, the single market officially opens.

1993   On May 18, 1993, Denmark approves the Maastricht treaty in a second referendum. The successful vote came after negotiations that will allow Denmark to opt out of the treaty's provisions for a common currency, central bank and defense policy. The only obstacle left for ratification of the treaty is the United Kingdom, who will debate it fervently through much of 1993, and hopefully accept it by late fall.

Glossary

Benelux countries: Belgium, the Netherlands and Luxembourg

CAP: see Common Agriculture Policy

Cecchini Report: A report published in 1988 under the title *Europe 1992—The overall Challenge* that provided an in depth economic analysis of the costs of Europe's fragmented marketplace. The study was conducted by a team led by Paolo Cecchini at the request of the EC Commission.

censure: see "motion of censure"

central bank: In simplest terms, a banker's bank; i.e. the source of loans for the banking system, which must be willing to lend to a qualified bank at anytime, though at its own terms. This gives it the ability to affect interest rates, and thereby influence the money supply of a country.

Commission: The executive branch of the EC legislative system. Responsible for proposing all new legislation, and overseeing Member States to be sure approved legislation is properly applied. Composed of 17 members (2 each from the 5 largest Member States, and one each from the 7 remaining). The Commission acts in the interest of the EC as a whole. All members of the Commission must commit to impartiality, and may not take directions from any national government. Headquartered in Brussels, Belgium.

Common Agriculture Policy: The policies adopted by the EC to provide support for the agricultural sector. Es-

sentially a subsidy program, its central feature is that it raises the income of the EC's farmers by keeping produce prices to the consumer high. This is basically accomplished by the EC Commission setting an "intervention" price for various commodities, and the Community buying into store to drive the price up whenever prices falls below the "intervention" price. Import prices are kept above the "intervention" price through import levies. About 70% of the EC budget is spent on agriculture support.

common market: see 'single market'

Constitutional Monarchy: A form of government in which a monarch, (i.e. a single individual), is the symbolic supreme ruler, yet a (generally written) constitution, which defines the set of principals according to which the country is organized, relieves the monarch of much of the responsibility and places power into bodies of elected or otherwise appointed individuals.

cooperation procedure: A procedure outlined in the Single European Act which is aimed at providing the European Parliament with more input into the legislative system. It requires a unanimous vote by the Council to approve legislation without modification when Parliament desires it be modified.

Council: The Council, or Council of Ministers, is the principal legislative and decision making institution in the EC system. The Council consists of one representative from each Member State (12 ministers total). Membership in the council varies by the subject under discussion, as each Member State generally sends their minister for that particular subject area, i.e., if finances are being discussed, each Member State is likely to send its finance minister to represent their interests. See also "European Council."

Court of Auditors: The institution responsible for auditing the accounts of all Community income and expense, including items that do not appear in the Community's budget. The results of the audit are published in annual and special reports. Membership consists of 12 individuals who are appointed for six years by the Council in consultation with the European Parliament. The Members of the Court of Auditors are completely independent in the performance of their duties.

Court of Justice: The EC's equivalent of a supreme court. It is the final judge of Community law. The Court has 13 judges, one from each Member Nation plus one to avoid the possibility of a tie vote.

currency flight: The practice of abandoning a national currency and conducting financial transactions in a foreign currency due to the advantages by the foreign currencies less volatile nature.

Decision: A class of legal instrument or "law" which is created by the EC legislative system. When acting under the Treaty of Rome (i.e. pertaining to the EEC or Euratom), a *Council Decision* is a legal instrument that is addressed toward a specific Member State government, firm or individual. It is binding in its entirety to those to whom it is addressed. Under the Treaty of Paris (i.e. pertaining to the

ECSC), a *Decision* is the strongest legal instrument issued by the system, and is binding in its entirety. See also "Regulations," "Directives," "Recommendations" and "Opinions."

DG: see Directorate-General

direct tax: A tax that is collected directly from a company's or individual's earnings. "Income tax" as known in the US is a *direct tax*.

Directive: A class of legal instruments or "laws" which are created by the EC legislative system. Used only when acting under the Treaty of Rome (i.e. pertaining to the EEC or Euratom), a *Council Directive* is addressed toward Member State governments and is binding as regards the results to be achieved, but leaves the method of achieving the results open to be decided by national authorities. See also "Regulations," "Decisions," "Recommendations" and "Opinions."

Directorate-General (DG): One of twenty-two area specific work groups under the European Commission, each of which has direct interaction with the commissioner assigned to that area.

duty: A payment due to a government, especially a tax on specific imports or exports like liquor or cigarettes.

EAGGF: see European Agriculture Guidance and Guarantee Fund

EC: see European Community

ECB: see European Central Bank

ECSC Treaty: see Treaty of Paris

ECSC: see European Coal and Steel Community

ECU: see European Currency Unit

EEA: see European Economic Area

EEC: see European Economic Community

EES: the European Economic Space, now commonly referred to as the European Economic Area (EEA)

EFTA: see European Free Trade Association

EIB: see European Investment Bank

EMI: see European Monetary Institute

EMS: see European Monetary System

EMU: see European Monetary Union

ERDF: see European Regional Development Fund

ERM: see Exchange Rate Mechanism

ESCB: see European System of Central Banks

ESF: see European Social Fund

EURATOM or Euratom: see European Atomic Energy Community

European Agriculture Guidance and Guarantee Fund: One of the four major funds administered by the Commission for the European Economic Community. The *European Agriculture Guidance and Guarantee Fund* provides funding for all provisions concerning agriculture subsidies and price supports.

European Atomic Energy Community (EURATOM): The third of the three European communities (ECSC, EEC, and Euratom). Established simultaneously with the European Economic Community (EEC) by the signing of the Treaty of Rome in 1957. Formed for the purpose of coordinating the development and distribution of atomic energy amongst its Member States.

European Central Bank (ECB): The European Community's independent central bank, as envisioned by the Treaty of Maastricht and its plan to implement European Monetary Union (EMU).

European Coal and Steel Community (ECSC): The first of the three European communities (ECSC, EEC and Euratom), and predecessor of today's EC. Formed in 1951 by the signing of the Treaty of Paris (which went into effect in July, 1952), the European Coal and Steel Community's purpose was to centrally manage the production of steel and coal. The signatories of the Treaty of Paris were Germany, France, Belgium, Italy, Luxembourg and the Netherlands, who became known as "the Six."

European Community (EC): The phrase commonly used when referring to the twelve European nations (Belgium, Denmark, France, Germany, Greece, Ireland, Italy, Luxembourg, Netherlands, Portugal, Spain and the United Kingdom) who have organized themselves through several treaties for purposes of increased cooperation on many fronts. Though 'European Community' is commonly used generically, there are actually *three*, distinct European Communities formed by individual treaties—the European Coal and Steel Community, the European Atomic Energy Community, and the European Economic Community. All three share the same institutions, which consist of the Council of Ministers, the Commission, The European Parliament, and the Court of Justice.

European Council: A special name for the gathering of the Heads of State or Government of each of the EC's twelve member states. The European Council has meet at least twice a year since 1974.

European Currency Unit (ECU): The

currency unit of the European Community, which presently exists alongside all of the EC's individual national currencies, and may eventually replace them. The ECU is comprised of "a basket" of national currencies, i.e. its value is determined by specific amounts of Member States' currencies; the more economically important having a larger share of the composition. Presently, it is possible to open a bank account denominated in ECUs, pay with ECU checks or buy ECU bonds, but the ECU is not yet a full fledged currency as no actual (other than symbolic) bills or coins have been issued. Issuance of actual ECU currency would follow successful completion of the European Monetary Union (EMU) plan. Should not be confused with the ancient French coin, the Ecu (eh-koo).

European currency snake: The name given to the arrangement which began in 1972 in which the countries of the EC agreed to manage their currencies in such a way that their respective exchange rates would remain within a narrow band in relation to one another. This was considered a necessary precondition for eventual monetary union. Each currency's exchange rate was allowed to fluctuate by only $\pm$ 2.5 % in relation to the other currencies. The snake was replaced by the European Monetary System (EMS) and its Exchange Rate Mechanism (ERM) in 1979.

European Development Fund: One of the four major funds administered by the Commission for the European Economic Community. The *European Development Fund* (EDF) is the EC's source of the foreign aid.

European Economic Area (EEA): The area resulting from the 1992 agreement between the EC and EFTA to extend the provisions of the Single European Act regarding the free movement of goods, capital, services and persons to the nations of EFTA, thereby creating a harmonized market of about 400 million consumers. Eventually, association with the emerging democracies of East Europe under the organization of the EEA is foreseen.

European Economic Community (EEC): An international organization created by the Treaty of Rome on March 25, 1957, to establish economic integration between its member states. Present member states are: Germany, France, Portugal, the Netherlands, Greece, Luxembourg, the United Kingdom, Italy, Belgium, Spain, Denmark and Ireland. In 1985 the Single European Act was initiated by the EEC to sufficiently deregulate its member states, and to harmonize necessary regulation, so as to allow the free movement of goods, people services and capital within its borders, by the end of 1992. The name EEC is to be officially changed by the Treaty of Maastricht (if ratified) to the European Community (EC), implying an organization of nations that is not only integrated economically, but also politically and socially.

European Economic Space (EES): The prior name for what is now commonly referred to as the European Economic Area.

European Free Trade Association (EFTA): An organization, presently of seven countries, Austria, Iceland, Finland, Norway, Sweden, Switzerland and Liechtenstein, whose aim is to achieve free trade in industrial goods between its member states, to help create a single West European market and to promote expansion in world trade. EFTA is the EC's most important trading partner, and the recent negotiation of a treaty linking their two economies (the European Economic Area or EEA) results in a combined market that represents almost 400 million consumers.

European Investment Bank (EIB): The EC's financial institution. It is a non-profit institution which raises funds by issuing bonds and other financial instruments on the financial markets, and then makes loans for investment which will contribute to the growth of the Community at an interest rate which reflects the cost of the funds. Its main objectives are the development of the less-developed regions of the Community and the construction of transport and communications infrastructures.

European Monetary Institute (EMI): A temporary institution defined in the Treaty of Maastricht in its plan to achieve European Monetary Union (EMU). The EMI would be the transitional authority on monetary policy during Stage II of EMU, and would be replaced by the European Central Bank (ECB) after the common currency, the ECU, is adopted. The EMI would be managed by a council consisting of the Governors of the national central banks.

European Monetary System (EMS): The system of common international financial structures adopted by the Member States of the EC in 1979. The essential elements of the EMS are the Exchange Rate Mechanism, which keeps the value of the various EC currencies within a narrow band of fluctuation, the European Currency Unit, the EC's currency, and the European Monetary Cooperation Fund, which is the clearing house for the Member States' Central Banks.

European Monetary Union (EMU): The agreement formalized by the Treaty of Maastricht to establish a single European currency by 1999. Under EMU, states would have to satisfy certain financial criteria before being allowed to join the union, and the currency, the ECU, would be managed by an independent central bank. The Maastricht Treaty calls for implementation of EMU in three successive stages.

European Regional Development Fund (ERDF): One of the four major funds administered by the Commission for the European Economic Community. The *European Regional Development Fund* provides funds for needed infrastructure improvements to alleviate imbalances within the community.

European Social Fund (ESF): One of the four major funds administered by the Commission for the European Economic Community. The *European Social Fund* provides money for vocational training for EC workers.

European System of Central Banks: The central banks of each Member State and the European Central Bank (ECB) collectively, as defined under the plan for European Monetary Union (EMU) in the Treaty of Maastricht. The ESCB would be created under Stage II of EMU, and must be established no later than July 1, 1998. Envisioned by the Treaty of Maastricht as a "Euro-Fed," whose responsibilities would be to establish price stability, support general, Community level economic policy, formulate and implement monetary policy, and coordinate banking supervision policies. Ultimately, the ESCB is responsible for coordinating policies such that the European Currency Unit (ECU) can replace the

12 individual national currencies by 1999.

Eurosclerosis: A term invented to describe the slowdown of European integration efforts between 1973 and 1984.

Exchange Rate Mechanism (ERM): A major element of the European Monetary System that is responsible for controlling the fluctuation of the exchange rates of the 12 national currencies of the EC's Member States. Similar to its predecessor, the European currency snake, ERM sets limits within which each currency's exchange rate may move relative to all the others. Presently, the EC currencies may fluctuate widely. The allowed band of fluctuation was increased from ± 2.25 % to ± 15 % in 1993 due to pressure from currency specualtion. This move is intended to be temporary. The ERM was initiated in 1979.

executive power: The authority within a government to put new laws into effect.

faux pas: a cultural blunder, *French*

federation: A country or other organization with a system of government in which several states (or group members) unite under a central authority, but remain independent in internal affairs.

fiscal barrier: Differences in tax rates between countries that necessitate border checks to ensure that appropriate taxes are paid.

GDP: see gross domestic product

GNP: see gross national product

gross domestic product (GDP): The gross national product (GNP) of a country less all income which accrued to domestic residents arising from investments and possessions in foreign countries over the period of one year.

gross national product: The total value of goods produced and services provided by a country in one year.

IMF: see International Monetary Fund

indirect tax: A tax which is collected on expenditures. "Sales tax" is an indirect tax whereby an individual may be required to pay, say 7%, of the price of an item to the government as a tax—if the individual does not buy the item, he avoids the tax. Thus, the amount of revenue a government receives from indirect taxation depends directly upon how much is consumed. Value-added tax is the primary source of indirect tax revenues in the EC.

internal market: As defined by the Single European Act, an area without internal frontiers (borders) in which the free movement of goods, persons, services and capital is ensured. See also 'single market.'

International Monetary Fund: A specialized agency of the United Nations. The International Monetary Fund's cause is to promote international monetary cooperation.

legislative power: The power to make laws.

Maastricht Treaty: The treaty signed in Maastricht, Netherlands, by representatives of each of the 12 EC Member States in December 1991, and officially titled "Treaty on European Union". Provides the necessary amendments to the Treaty of Rome to enable political union and economic and monetary union to be achieved, as well as fostering a common foreign policy and introducing a common citizenship. The treaty's most explicitly defined sections deal with the implementation of European Monetary Union

(EMU) and the adoption of a single currency.

market: For the purposes of this book, a market may be thought of as the collection of selling opportunities available to a business. A national market is expressed in terms of population, as each person represents a potential customer.

Marshall Plan: The post World War II plan sponsored by the United States to provide Europe with the funds necessary to recover from the immense damage caused by the war. Officially called the European Recovery Program. Named after the US Secretary of State in 1947, General G. C. Marshall.

member state (or member nation): Any of the 12 individual nations which together make up the European Community.

MEP: Member of the European Parliament; the acronym name assigned to members of the European Parliament.

Merger Treaty: The treaty signed in Brussels in 1965 which replaced the three separate Councils and Commissions of the ECSC, the EEC, and Euratom with a single Council and a single Commission which assume all of the powers and responsibilities previously held by their predecessors, thereby creating the single European Community (EC) which is spoken of today.

motion of censure: A formal proposal of strong criticism and dissatisfaction with performance. Parliament has the sole ability to dismiss the Commission by adopting a "motion of censure," by at least a two-thirds majority.

OECD: see Organization for Economic Cooperation and Development

OEEC: see Organization for European Economic Cooperation

Opinion: A class of legal instrument or "law" which is created by the EC legislative system. When acting under either the Treaty of Rome (i.e. pertaining to the EEC or Euratom), or the Treaty of Paris (i.e. pertaining to the ECSC), an *Opinion* is a legal instrument that is not binding, but serves as advice to those to which it is directed. See also "Regulations," "Directives," "Decisions," and "Recommendations."

Organization for Economic Cooperation and Development (OECD): An international organization which replaced the post World War II Organization for European Economic Cooperation. Its purpose is to encourage economic growth and high employment with financial stability in member states and to contribute to the economic development of the worlds less advanced countries and the expansion of world multilateral trade. Headquartered in Paris, France. Member Nations include all nations of the EC and EFTA, as well as the USA, Canada, Australia, New Zealand, and Turkey. Yugoslavia has observer status.

Organization for European Economic Cooperation (OEEC): An organization, consisting of 16 Western European countries, which was formed in 1947, just after World War II, as part of the Marshall Aid Plan. The purpose of the OEEC was to reestablish trade between the countries of Europe. In 1961, in light of its expanding role, the name of the OEEC was changed to the Organization for Economic Cooperation and Development (OECD), which includes the USA and Canada as full members.

Parliament (European Parliament): The second legislative body of the EC system, consisting of 518 elected (by EC citizens) members. The Parliament meets in Strasbourg, France, and members associate themselves by political party within the Parliament regardless of nationality. Serves primarily as a consultative body, with some ability to amend draft legislation.

physical barrier: Border controls, immigration checks, baggage searches and other obstructions that "physically" interrupt the movement of people and goods. See also "technical barrier" and "fiscal barrier," which are the primary reasons physical barriers were established.

plenary session: A session, or meeting of a group at which all members are present.

protectionism: The policy of protecting domestic industries by restricting and/or adding taxes to imports in order to discourage foreign competition.

Qualified Majority Voting: A system of voting adopted in February 1987 as part of the Single European Act to expedite the decision making process of the Council. Under the system, 54 of a possible 76 votes (71%) are required for approval of a proposal. Each Member State is given a defined number of votes based on its population. The system makes it impossible for any single country or pair of countries to prevent a proposal from being approved, while at the same time, it requires that at least two large countries vote for a particular proposal in order for it to be approved.

Recommendation: A class of legal instrument or "law" which is created by the EC legislative system. When acting under the Treaty of Rome (i.e. pertaining to the EEC or Euratom), a *Council Recommendation* is a legal instrument functionally the same as an *Opinion* that is not binding, but serves as advice to those to which it is directed. Under the Treaty of Paris (i.e., pertaining to the ECSC), a *Recommendation* is binding as regards the results to be achieved, but open concerning the method used to obtain the results. See also "Regulations," "Directives," "Decisions," and "Opinions."

Regulation: A class of legal instrument or "law" which is created by the EC legislative system. Only applicable when acting under the Treaty of Rome (i.e. pertaining to the EEC or Euratom), a *Council Regulation* is the strongest legal instrument adopted, and is binding in its entirety to all Member States. See also "Directives," "Decisions," "Recommendations" and "Opinions."

republic: A country in which the foremost power is held by the people or by their elected representatives.

Schengen Agreement: An accord to abolish customs and immigration controls at the common borders of Luxembourg, France, Germany, the Netherlands, Belgium and Italy. The Agreement was originally signed in Schengen, Luxembourg, in June 1990 by five of the six present participants, Italy signing on later in that year. The treaty was to become effectual in 1992. Spain and Portugal have observer status, and expected to eventually join in the Agreement.

Schuman Declaration (or Schuman Plan): The plan put forth in 1950 by the then foreign minister of France to establish an organization to manage European coal and steel production. This led to the formation of the European Coal and Steel Community, the predecessor of today's European Community.

secretariat: Refers to all of the members of a government administrative office taken as one.

Single European Act (Single Act): The most significant amendment ever made to the Community's Treaties. It was adopted as a means to help expedite the passage of legislation necessary to achieve the common internal market outlined in the "White Paper." It came into force July 1, 1987, making such provisions as establishing the system of qualified majority voting, and giving the Commission the power to investigate and determine if national laws met Community requirements. Nations not in compliance could be asked to change their laws to comply with EC law. Further, it gave Parliament additional say in the legislative process by granting it "power of assent" on proposed legislation.

single European market: see 'single market'

single market: The name generally used for the European Community's efforts to deregulate itself such that people, goods, money and services are free to move about within the EC without unnecessary restrictions. The single market is also referred to as 'the internal market,' the 'common market' or the 'Single European Market.'

Six, the: "The Six" refers to the original signatories of the Treaty of Paris, which were Germany, France, Belgium, Italy, Luxembourg and the Netherlands.

Snake, the: see European currency snake

sovereign: A king or queen who is supreme ruler of a country.

subsidiarity: The principle that the European Community should act only in areas that it is able to deal with more effectively than the Member States acting alone. The principal of subsidiarity is applied, for example, in research and technological development (to reduce unnecessary repetition of effort), which can be more efficiently run by a central organization, and is therefore administered in Brussels. Other areas, such as allocation of national budgets, are obviously better left in the hands of the Member States. This principal has become very important in limiting public fears that too much power will be transferred to Brussels.

tariff: A tax charged on certain goods when imported or exported.

technical barriers: Differences in specifications or required standards that make it difficult for a company to sell a uniform product throughout the EC. For example Italy once required all pasta to made of 100% durum wheat; many pastas from other countries were not made of 100% durum flour, and thus could not be sold in Italy.

Treaty of Paris: The treaty signed in April 1951 in Paris by "the Six" original members of the EC; Germany, France, Belgium, Italy, Luxembourg and the Netherlands, which established the European Coal and Steel Community.

Treaty of Rome: The treaty officially entitled the "Treaty establishing the European Economic Community." Signed in 1957, the Treaty of Rome created the EEC and Euratom, and remains the basic underlying document of today's EC.

UN: see United Nations

United Nations: A general international organization for the maintenance of international peace and security consisting of 158 member nations.

Value-added tax (VAT):   Tax on the amount by which the value of an article has been increased at each stage of its production. For example, if a company buys hops and barley for $1 and produces beer which it sells for $3, a VAT tax would be applied to the $2 difference.

VAT: see Value-added tax

White Paper: The program and timetable for the completion of the single European market. Entitled "Completing the Internal Market," it was published by the Commission in June 1985 and set forth all the actions necessary to achieve the common market by December 31, 1992. (note: a "White Paper," which is a British term, in general refers to any official government report—originally they were bound in the same white paper as the pages).

World Bank: A specialized agency of the United Nations whose aim is to encourage development through capital investment, particularly in poorer member nations of the UN. Headquartered in Washington DC, USA and officially titled "International Bank for Reconstruction and Development."

Index

Page references in **boldface** indicate Glossary terms.

227

Order Form

Additional copies of this book may be obtained easily.

Telephone Orders: call 1-800-247-6553. Please have your credit card ready.

Postal Orders: Send order blank below with a check or money order to:

BookMasters, Inc.
Distributor for Stone & Quill Publishing
P.O. Box 2039
Mansfield, OH 44905

Fax Orders: dial (419) 281-6883. Send order blank below.

Please send me the following copies of:

The European Community:
An Essential Guide Toward Knowing and Understanding the EC

		Quantity	Amount
Hardcover	$25.95	( )	$_____
Softcover	$15.95	( )	$_____
	Subtotal		$_____
	Shipping (see below)*		$_____
	TOTAL ENCLOSED		$_____

*Shipping:

Book Rate: $2.00 for the first book and 75 cents for each additional book.
(Surface Shipping may take three to four weeks)

Airmail: $3.50 per book

Ship to:

Company Name _____
Name _____
Address _____
City _____ State _____ Zip _____

Payment: ☐ Check   ☐ Credit Card (Exp. date____/____)
                                        ☐ Visa   ☐ Mastercard

Card Number _____ Name on Card _____

Signature _____